Mathe

# Equations of the Second Degree

## A Selection of Classic Mathematical Articles Containing Examples and Exercises on the Subject of Algebra

### By

### Various Authors

**British Library Cataloguing-in-Publication Data**
A catalogue record for this book is available from
the British Library

# Contents

**110.** Equations of the second degree may involve *but one* unknown quantity, or they may involve *more than one*. We shall first consider the former class.

**111.** An equation containing but one unknown quantity is said to be of the *second degree*, when the highest power of the unknown quantity in any term, is the second.

Let us assume the equation,

$$\frac{a}{b}x^2 - cx + d = cx^2 + \frac{b}{d}x + a.$$

Clearing of fractions,

$$adx^2 - bcdx + bd^2 = bcdx^2 + b^2x + abd;$$

transposing, $\quad adx^2 - bcdx^2 - bcdx - b^2x = abd - bd^2;$

factoring, $\quad (ad - bcd)x^2 - (bcd + b^2)x = abd - bd^2;$

dividing both members by the co-efficient of $x^2$,

$$x^2 - \frac{bcd + b^2}{ad - bcd}x = \frac{abd - bd^2}{ad - bcd}.$$

If we now replace the co-efficient of $x$ by $2p$, and the second member by $q$, we shall have

$$x^2 + 2px = q;$$

and since every equation of the second degree may be reduced. in like manner, we conclude that, every equation of the second degree, involving but one unknown quantity, can be reduced to the form

$$x^2 + 2px = q,$$

by the following

1

## RULE.

I. *Clear the equation of fractions;*

II. *Transpose all the known terms to the second member, and all the unknown terms to the first.*

III. *Reduce the terms involving the square of the unknown quantity to a single term of two factors, one of which is the square of the unknown quantity;*

IV. *Then, divide both members by the co-efficient of the square of the unknown quantity.*

**112.** If $2p$, the algebraic sum of the co-efficients of the first powers of $x$, becomes equal to 0, the equation will take the form

$$x^2 = q,$$

and this is called, an *incomplete equation* of the second degree. Hence,

*An incomplete equation of the second degree involves only the second power of the unknown quantity and known terms, and may be reduced to the form*

$$x^2 \doteq q.$$

### Solution of Incomplete Equations.

**113.** Having reduced the equation to the required form, we have simply *to extract the square root of both members to find the value of the unknown quantity.*

Extracting the square root of both members of the equation

$$x^2 = q, \quad \text{we have} \quad x = \sqrt{q}.$$

If $q$ is a perfect square, the exact value of $x$ can be found by extracting the square root of $q$, and the value of $x$ will then be expressed either algebraically or in numbers.

If $q$ is an algebraic quantity, and not a perfect square, it must be reduced to its simplest form by the rules for reducing radicals of the second degree. If $q$ is a number, and not a perfect square, its square root must be determined, approximately, by the rules already given.

2

But the *square* of any number is $+$, whether the number itself have the $+$ or $-$ sign: hence, it follows that

$$(+\sqrt{q})^2 = q, \quad \text{and} \quad (-\sqrt{q})^2 = q;$$

and therefore, the unknown quantity $x$ is susceptible of two distinct values, viz :

$$x = +\sqrt{q}, \quad \text{and} \quad x = -\sqrt{q};$$

and either of these values, being substituted for $x$, will satisfy the given equation. For,

$$x^2 = +\sqrt{q} \times +\sqrt{q} = q;$$

and
$$x^2 = -\sqrt{q} \times -\sqrt{q} = q; \quad \text{hence,}$$

*Every incomplete equation of the second degree has two roots which are numerically equal to each other; one having the sign plus, and the other the sign minus* (Art. 77).

EXAMPLES.

1. Let us take the equation

$$\frac{1}{3}x^2 - 3 + \frac{5}{12}x^2 = \frac{7}{24} - x^2 + \frac{299}{24}.$$

which, by making the terms entire, becomes

$$8x^2 - 72 + 10x^2 = 7 - 24x^2 + 299,$$

and by transposing and reducing

$$42x^2 = 378 \quad \text{and} \quad x^2 = \frac{378}{42} = 9;$$

hence, $\quad x = +\sqrt{9} = +3;$ and $\quad x = -\sqrt{9} = -3.$

2. As a second example, let us take the equation

$$3x^2 = 5.$$

Dividing both members by 3 and extracting the square root,

$$x = \pm\sqrt{\frac{5}{3}} = \pm\frac{1}{3}\sqrt{15};$$

in which the values of $x$ must be determined approximately

3. What are the values of $x$ in the equation

$$11(x^2 - 4) = 5(x^2 + 2). \qquad Ans. \ x = \pm 3.$$

4. What are the values of $x$ in the equation

$$\frac{\sqrt{m^2 - x^2}}{x} = n. \qquad Ans \ x = \pm \frac{m}{\sqrt{1 + n^2}}$$

3

*Solution of Equations of the Second Degree.*

114. Let us now solve the equation of the second degree

$$x^2 + 2px = q.$$

If we compare the first member with the square of

$$x + p, \quad \text{which is} \quad x^2 + 2px + p^2,$$

we see, that it needs but the square of $p$ to render it a perfect square. If then, $p^2$ be added to the first member, it will become a perfect square; but in order to preserve the equality of the members, $p^2$ must also be added to the second member. Making these additions, we have

$$x^2 + 2px + p^2 = q + p^2;$$

this is called, *completing the square*, and is done, *by adding the square of half the co-efficient of $x$ to both members of the equation.*

Now, if we extract the square root of both members, we have,

$$x + p = \pm\sqrt{q + p^2},$$

and by transposing $p$, we shall have

$$x = -p + \sqrt{q + p^2}, \quad \text{and} \quad x = -p - \sqrt{q + p^2}.$$

Either of these values, being substituted for $x$ in the equation

$$x^2 + 2px = q$$

will satisfy it. For, substituting the first value,

$$x^2 = (-p + \sqrt{q + p^2})^2 = p^2 - 2p\sqrt{q + p^2} + q + p^2,$$

and

$$2px = 2p \times (-p + \sqrt{q + p^2}) = -2p^2 + 2p\sqrt{q + p^2},$$
$$\text{by adding} \quad x^2 + 2px = q.$$

Substituting the second value of $x$, we find,

$$x^2 = (-p - \sqrt{q + p^2})^2 = p^2 + 2p\sqrt{q + p^2} + q + p^2.$$

and

$$2px = 2p(-p - \sqrt{q + p^2}) = -2p^2 - 2p\sqrt{q + p^2};$$
$$\text{by adding} \quad x^2 + 2px = q;$$

and consequently, both values found above, are *roots* of the equation.

EQUATIONS OF THE SECOND DEGREE.

In order to refer readily, to either of these which we shall call the one which arises from using the $+$ sign before the radical, the *first value* of $x$, or the *first root* of the equation; and the other, the *second value* of $x$, or the *second root* of the equation.

Having reduced a complete equation of the second degree to the form

$$x^2 + 2px = q,$$

we can write immediately the two values of the unknown quantity by the following

### RULE.

I. *The first value of the unknown quantity is equal to half the co-efficient of $x$, taken with a contrary sign, plus the square root of the second member increased by the square of half this co-efficient.*

II. *The second value is equal to half the co-efficient of $x$, taken with a contrary sign, minus the square root of the second member increased by the square of half this co-efficient.*

#### EXAMPLES.

1. Let us take as an example,
$$x^2 - 7x + 10 = 0.$$
Reducing to required form,
$$x^2 - 7x = -10;$$
whence by the rule, $x = \dfrac{7}{2} + \sqrt{-10 + \dfrac{49}{4}} = 5;$

and, $\qquad x = \dfrac{7}{2} - \sqrt{-10 + \dfrac{49}{4}} = 2.$

2. As a second example, let us take the equation
$$\frac{5}{6}x^2 - \frac{1}{2}x + \frac{3}{4} = 8 - \frac{2}{3}x - x^2 + \frac{273}{12}.$$

5

Reducing to the required form, we have,

$$x^2 + \frac{2}{22}x = \frac{360}{22};$$

whence,
$$x = -\frac{1}{22} + \sqrt{\frac{360}{22} + \left(\frac{1}{22}\right)^2}$$

and
$$x = -\frac{1}{22} - \sqrt{\frac{360}{22} + \left(\frac{1}{22}\right)^2}.$$

It often occurs, in the solution of equations, that $p^2$ and $q$ are fractions, as in the above example. These fractions most generally arise from dividing by the co-efficient of $x^2$ in the reduction of the equation to the required form. When this is the case, we readily discover the quantity by which it is necessary to multiply the term $q$, in order to reduce it to the same denominator with $p^2$; after which, the numerators may be added together and placed over the common denominator. After this operation, the denominator will be a perfect square, and may be brought from under the radical sign, and will become a divisor of the square root of the numerator.

To apply these principles in reducing the radical part of the values of $x$, in the last example, we have

$$\pm\sqrt{\frac{360}{22} + \left(\frac{1}{22}\right)^2} = \pm\sqrt{\frac{360 \times 22}{(22)^2} + \frac{1}{(22)^2}} = \pm\sqrt{\frac{7920 + 1}{(22)^2}}$$

$$= \pm\frac{1}{22}\sqrt{7921} = \pm\frac{89}{22};$$

and therefore, the two values of $x$ become,

$$x = -\frac{1}{22} + \frac{89}{22} = \frac{88}{22} = 4;$$

and
$$x = -\frac{1}{22} - \frac{89}{2} = -\frac{90}{22} = -\frac{45}{11};$$

either of which being substituted for $x$ in the given equation, will satisfy it.

3. What are the values of $x$ in the equation.

$$ax^2 - ac = cx - bx^2.$$

Reducing to required form, we have,

$$x^2 - \frac{c}{a+b}x = \frac{ac}{a+b};$$

whence, $x = + \frac{c}{2(a+b)} + \sqrt{\frac{ac}{a+b} + \frac{c^2}{4(a+b)^2}},$

and, $x = + \frac{c}{2(a+b)} - \sqrt{\frac{ac}{a+b} + \frac{c^2}{4(a+b)^2}}.$

Reducing the terms under the radical sign to a common denominator, we find,

$$\sqrt{\frac{ac}{a+b} + \frac{c^2}{4(a+b)^2}} = \sqrt{\frac{4a^2c + 4abc + c^2}{4(a+b)^2}} = \frac{\sqrt{4a^2c + 4abc + c^2}}{2(a+b)};$$

hence, $x = \frac{c \pm \sqrt{4a^2c + 4abc + c^2}}{2(a+b)}.$

4. What are the values of $x$, in the equation,

$$6x^2 - 37x = -57.$$

By reducing to the required form, we have,

$$x^2 - \frac{37}{6}x = -\frac{57}{6};$$

whence, $x = + \frac{37}{12} \pm \sqrt{-\frac{57}{6} + \left(\frac{37}{12}\right)^2}$

Reducing the quantities under the radical sign to a common denominator, we have,

$$x = + \frac{37}{12} \pm \sqrt{\frac{-114 \times 12}{(12)^2} + \frac{(37)^2}{(12)^2}}.$$

But, $114 \times 12 = 1368$; and $(37)^2 = 1369$;

hence, $x = + \frac{37}{12} \pm \sqrt{\frac{-1368 + 1369}{(12)^2}} = + \frac{37}{12} \pm \frac{1}{12};$

or, $x = + \frac{37}{12} + \frac{1}{12} = \frac{19}{6},$

and, $x = + \frac{37}{12} - \frac{1}{12} = 3.$

5. What are the values of $x$, in the equation,

$$4a^2 - 2x^2 + 2ax = 18ab - 18b^2.$$

7

Reducing to the required form, we have,

$$x^2 - ax = 2a^2 - 9ab + 9b^2;$$

whence,

$$x = \frac{a}{2} \pm \sqrt{2a^2 - 9ab + 9b^2 + \frac{a^2}{4}}$$

$$= \frac{a}{2} \pm \sqrt{\frac{9a^2}{4} - 9ab + 9b^2}.$$

The radical part is equal to $\frac{3a}{2} - 3b$; hence,

$$x = \frac{a}{2} \pm \left(\frac{3a}{2} - 3b\right); \quad \text{or} \quad \begin{cases} x = 2a - 3b. \\ x = -a + 3b. \end{cases}$$

Find the values of $x$ in the following

### EXAMPLES.

1. $\dfrac{x^2}{3} - \dfrac{a}{b}x = 1 - \dfrac{b}{a}x - \dfrac{2x^2}{3}.$  *Ans.* $x = \dfrac{a}{b}, \quad x = -\dfrac{b}{a}.$

2. $\dfrac{dx}{c} + \dfrac{3x^2}{4} + 1 = \dfrac{1+c}{c} - \dfrac{x^2}{4} + \dfrac{x}{d}.$

   *Ans.* $x = \dfrac{1}{d}, \quad x = -\dfrac{d}{c}$

3. $\dfrac{x^2}{4} - \dfrac{2x}{3} + \dfrac{59}{8} = 8 - \dfrac{x^2}{4} - \dfrac{x}{3}.$

   *Ans.* $x = \dfrac{3}{2}, \quad x = -\dfrac{5}{6}$

4. $\dfrac{90}{x} - \dfrac{90}{x+1} = \dfrac{27}{x+2}.$  *Ans.* $x = 4, \quad x = -\dfrac{5}{3}$

5. $\dfrac{2x-10}{8-x} - 2 = \dfrac{x+3}{x-2}.$  *Ans.* $x = 7, \quad x = \dfrac{4}{5}.$

6. $ax - \dfrac{x^2}{b} + b = \dfrac{b-1}{b}x^2 + \dfrac{b}{a}x.$  *Ans.* $x = a, \quad x = -\dfrac{b}{a}.$

7. $\dfrac{a-b}{c}x + \dfrac{3x^2}{2} - \dfrac{a^2}{c^2} = \dfrac{b+a}{c}x + \dfrac{x^2}{2} - \dfrac{b^2}{c^2}.$

   *Ans.* $x = \dfrac{b+a}{c}, \quad x = \dfrac{b-a}{c}.$

8. $mx^2 + mn = 2m\sqrt{n}\,x + nx^2.$

$$Ans. \quad x = \frac{\sqrt{mn}}{\sqrt{m} - \sqrt{n}}, \quad x = -\frac{\sqrt{mn}}{\sqrt{m} + \sqrt{n}}.$$

9. $abx^2 - \dfrac{6a^2}{c^2} + \dfrac{b^2x}{c} = \dfrac{ab - 2b^2}{c^2} - \dfrac{3a^2}{c}x.$

$$Ans. \quad x = \frac{2a - b}{ac}, \quad x = -\frac{3a + 2b}{bc}.$$

10 $\dfrac{4x^2}{7} + \dfrac{2x}{7} + 10 = 19 - \dfrac{3x^2}{7} + \dfrac{58x}{7}.$

$$Ans. \quad x = 9, \quad x = -1.$$

11. $\dfrac{x + a}{x - a} - b = \dfrac{a - x}{a + x}.$  $\qquad Ans. \quad x = \pm a\sqrt{\dfrac{b + 2}{b - 2}}.$

12. $2x + 2 = 24 - 5x - 2x^2.$  $\qquad Ans. \quad x = 2, \quad x = -\dfrac{11}{2}.$

13. $x^2 - x - 40 = 170.$  $\qquad Ans. \quad x = 15, \text{ and } x = -14.$

14. $3x^2 + 2x - 9 = 76.$  $\qquad Ans. \quad x = 5, \text{ and } x = -5\frac{2}{3}.$

15. $a^2 + b^2 - 2bx + x^2 = \dfrac{m^2 t^2}{n^2}.$

$$Ans. \quad x = \frac{n}{n^2 - n}(bn \pm \sqrt{a^2 m^2 + b^2 m^2 - a^2 n^2}).$$

*Problems giving rise to Equations of the Second Degree involv-*
*ing but one unknown quantity.*

1. Find a number such that three times the number added to
twice its square will be equal to 65.

Let $x$ denote the number. Then from the conditions,

$$2x^2 + 3x = 65 \quad \cdot \quad \cdot \quad \cdot \quad (1)$$

Whence, $\qquad x = -\dfrac{3}{4} \pm \sqrt{\dfrac{65}{2} + \dfrac{9}{16}};$

reducing $\qquad x = 5 \text{ and } x = -\dfrac{13}{2}.$

Both of these roots verify the equation: for,

$$2 \times (5)^2 + 3 \times 5 = 2 \times 25 + 15 = 65;$$

and $\quad 2\left(-\dfrac{13}{2}\right)^2 + 3 \times -\dfrac{13}{2} = \dfrac{169}{2} - \dfrac{39}{2} = \dfrac{130}{2} = 65.$

The first root satisfies the conditions of the problem as enunciated.

The second root will also satisfy the conditions, if we regard its algebraic sign. Had we denoted the unknown quantity by $-x$, we should have found

$$2x^2 - 3x = 65 \quad \cdots \quad (2)$$

from which $\quad\quad x = \dfrac{13}{2}$ and $x = -5.$

We see that the roots of this equation differ from those of equation (1) only in their signs, a result which was to have been expected, since we can change equation (1) into equation (2) by simply changing the sign of $x$, and the reverse.

2. A person purchased a number of yards of cloth for 240 cents. If he had received three yards less, for the same sum, it would have cost him 4 cents more per yard. How many yards did he purchase?

Let $x$ denote the number of yards purchased.

Then will $\dfrac{240}{x}$ denote the number of cents paid per yard.

Had he received three yards less,

$x - 3$, would have denoted the number of yards purchased, and $\dfrac{240}{x-3}$, would have denoted the number of cents he paid per yard.

From the conditions of the problem,

$$\dfrac{240}{x-3} - \dfrac{240}{x} = 4;$$

by reducing, $\quad\quad x^2 - 3x = 180,$

whence, $\quad\quad x = 15$ and $x = -12.$

The value $x = 15$ satisfies the conditions of the problem, understood in their arithmetical sense; for. 15 yards for 240

10

cents, gives $\dfrac{240}{15}$, or 16 cents for the price of one yard, and 12 yards for 240 cents, gives 20 cents for the price of one yard, which exceeds 16 by 4.

The value $+ x = -12$, or $-x = +12$, will satisfy the conditions of the following problem:

*A person sold a number of yards of cloth for 240 cents: if he had received the same sum for 3 yards more, it would have brought him 4 cents less per yard. How many yards did he sell?*

If we denote the number of yards sold by $x$, the statement of this last problem, and the given one, both give rise to the same equation,

$$x^2 - 3x = 180,$$

hence, the solution of this equation ought to give the answers to both problems, as we see that it does.

Generally, when the solution of the equation of a problem gives two roots, if the problem does not admit of two solutions there is always another problem whose statement gives rise to the same equation as the given one, and in this case the two roots form answers to both problems.

3. A man bought a horse, which he sold for 24 dollars. At the sale, he lost as much per cent. on the price of his purchase, as the horse cost him. What did he pay for the horse?

Let $x$ denote the number of dollars that he paid for the horse: then, $x - 24$ will denote the number of dollars that he lost.

But as he lost $x$ per cent. by the sale, he must have lost $\dfrac{x}{100}$ upon each dollar, and upon $x$ dollars he lost a number of dollars denoted by $\dfrac{x^2}{100}$; we have then the equation

$$\frac{x^2}{100} = x - 24, \quad \text{whence} \quad x^2 - 100x = -2400;$$

Therefore, $x = 60$ and $x = 40$.

Both of these values satisfy the conditions of the problem.

11

For, in the first place, suppose the man gave 60 dollars for the horse and sold him for 24, he then loses 36 dollars. But, from the enunciation, he should lose 60 *per cent.* of 60, that is,

$$\frac{60}{100} \text{ of } 60 = \frac{60 \times 60}{100} = 36;$$

therefore, 60 satisfies the problem.

If he pays 40 dollars for the horse, he loses 16 by the sale; for, he should lose 40 *per cent.* of 40, or

$$40 \times \frac{40}{100} = 16;$$

therefore, 40 satisfies the conditions of the problem.

4. A grazier bought as many sheep as cost him £60, and after reserving 15 out of the number, he sold the remainder for £54, and gained 2*s.* a head on those he sold: how many did he buy?                                *Ans.* 75.

5. A merchant bought cloth for which he paid £33 15*s.*, which he sold again at £2 8*s.* per piece, and gained by the bargain as much as one piece cost him: how many pieces did he buy?
*Ans.* 15.

6. What number is that, which, being divided by the product of its digits, the quotient will be 3; and if 18 be added to it, the order of its digits will be reversed?     *Ans.* 24.

7. Find a number such that if you subtract it from 10, and multiply the remainder by the number itself, the product will be 21.                                    *Ans.* 7 or 3.

8. Two persons, A and B, departed from different places at the same time, and traveled towards each other. On meeting, it appeared that A had traveled 18 miles more than B; and that A could have performed B's journey in $15\frac{3}{4}$ days, but B would have been 28 days in performing A's journey. How far did each travel?

*Ans.* $\left\{\begin{array}{l} \text{A 72 miles.} \\ \text{B 54 miles.} \end{array}\right.$

9. A company at a tavern had £8 15*s.* to pay for their reckoning; but before the bill was settled, two of them left

the room, and then those who remained had 10s. apiece more to pay than before: how many were there in the company? *Ans.* 7.

10. What two numbers are those whose difference is 15, and of which the cube of the lesser is equal to half their product? *Ans.* 3 and 18.

11. Two partners, A and B, gained $140 in trade: A's money was 3 months in trade, and his gain was $60 less than his -tock: B's money was $50 more than A's, and was in trade 5 months: what was A's stock? *Ans.* $100.

12. Two persons, A and B, start from two different points, and travel toward each other. When they meet, it appears that A has traveled 30 miles more than B. It also appears that it will take A 4 days to travel the road that B had come, and B 9 days to travel the road that A had come. What was their distance apart when they set out? *Ans.* 150 miles.

*Discussion of Equations of the Second Degree involving but one unknown quantity.*

115. It has been shown that every complete equation of the second degree can be reduced to the form (Art. 113)

$$x^2 + 2px = q \quad - \ - \ - \quad (1),$$

in which $p$ and $q$ are numerical or algebraic, entire or fractional, and their signs plus or minus.

If we make the first member a perfect square, by completing the square (Art. 112*), we have

$$x^2 + 2px + p^2 = q + p^2,$$

which may be put under the form

$$(x + p)^2 = q + p^2.$$

Now, whatever may be the value of $q + p^2$, its square root may be represented by $m$, and the equation put under the form

$$(x + p)^2 = m^2, \quad \text{and consequently,} \quad (x + p)^2 - m^2 = 0.$$

13

But, as the first member of the last equation is the difference between two squares, it may be put under the form

$$(x + p - m)(x + p + m) = 0 \quad \cdots \quad (2),$$

in which the first member is the product of two factors, and the second 0. Now, we can make this product equal to 0, and consequently satisfy equation (2) only in two different ways: viz., by making

$$x + p - m = 0, \quad \text{whence,} \quad x = -p + m,$$

or, by making

$$x + p + m = 0, \quad \text{whence,} \quad x = -p - m.$$

Now, either of these values being substituted for $x$ in equation (2), will satisfy that equation, and consequently, will satisfy equation (1), from which it was derived. Hence, we conclude,

1st. *That every equation of the second degree has two roots, and only two.*

2d. *That the first member of every equation of the second degree, whose second member is 0, can be resolved into two binomial factors of the first degree with respect to the unknown quantity, having the unknown quantity for a first term and the two roots, with their signs changed, for second terms.*

For example, the equation

$$x^2 + 3x - 28 = 0$$

being solved, gives

$$x = 4 \quad \text{and} \quad x = -7;$$

either of which values will satisfy the equation. We also have

$$(x - 4)(x + 7) = x^2 + 3x - 28 = 0.$$

If the roots of an equation are known, we can readily form the binomial factors and deduce the equation.

### EXAMPLES.

1. What are the factors, and what is the equation, of which the roots are 8 and $-9$?

*Ans.* $x - 8$ and $x + 9$ are the binomial factors.

and $x^2 + x - 72 = 0$ is the equation.

14

2. What are the factors, and what is the equation, of which the roots are $-1$ and $+1$?

$$x + 1 \quad \text{and} \quad x - 1 \quad \text{are the factors,}$$
and $\qquad x^2 - 1 = 0 \qquad$ is the equation.

3. What are the factors, and what is the equation, whose roots are

$$\frac{7 + \sqrt{-1039}}{16} \quad \text{and} \quad \frac{7 - \sqrt{-1039}}{16} ?$$

*Ans.* $\left( x - \dfrac{7 + \sqrt{-1039}}{16} \right) \quad$ and $\quad \left( x - \dfrac{7 - \sqrt{-1039}}{16} \right)$

are the factors,

and $\qquad 8x^2 - 7x + 34 = 0 \quad$ is the equation.

116. If we designate the two roots, found in the preceding article, by $x'$ and $x''$, we shall have,

$$x' = -p + m,$$
$$x'' = -p - m;$$

or substituting for $m$ its value $\sqrt{q + p^2}$,

$$x' = -p + \sqrt{q + p^2},$$
$$x'' = -p - \sqrt{q + p^2}.$$

Adding these equations, member to member, we get

$$x' + x'' = -2p;$$

and multiplying them, member by member, and reducing, we find

$$x' x'' = -q.$$

Hence, after an equation has been reduced to the form of

$$x^2 + 2px = q,$$

1st. *The algebraic sum of its two roots is equal to the co-efficient of the first power of the unknown quantity, with its sign changed.*

2d. *The product of the two roots is equal to the second member, with its sign changed.*

If the sum of two quantities is given or known, their product will be the greatest possible when they are equal.

Let $2p$ be the sum of two quantities, and denote their difference by $2d$; then,

$p + d$ will denote the greater, and $p - d$ the less quantity. If we represent their product by $q$, we shall have

$$p^2 - d^2 = q.$$

Now, it is plain that $q$ will increase as $d$ diminishes, and that it will be the greatest possible, when $d = 0$; that is, when the two quantities are equal to each other, in which case the product becomes equal to $p^2$. Hence,

3d. *The greatest possible value of the product of the two roots, is equal to the square of half the co-efficient of the first power of the unknown quantity.*

## Of the Four Forms.

117. Thus far, we have regarded $p$ and $q$ as algebraic quantities, without considering the essential sign of either, nor have we at all regarded their relative values.

If we first suppose $p$ and $q$ to be both essentially positive, then to become negative in succession, and after that, both to become negative together, we shall have all the combinations of signs which can arise. The complete equation of the second degree will, therefore, always be expressed under one of the four following forms:—

$$x^2 + 2px = \quad q \quad (1),$$
$$x^2 - 2px = \quad q \quad (2),$$
$$x^2 + 2px = -\,q \quad (3),$$
$$x^2 - 2px = -\,q \quad (4).$$

These equations being solved, give

$$x = -\,p \pm \sqrt{\quad q + p^2} \quad (1),$$
$$x = +\,p \pm \sqrt{\quad q + p^2} \quad (2),$$
$$x = -\,p \pm \sqrt{-\,q + p^2} \quad (3),$$
$$x = +\,p \pm \sqrt{-\,q + p^2} \quad (4).$$

In the first and second forms, the quantity under the radical sign will be positive, whatever be the relative values of $p$ and $q$, since $q$ and $p^2$ are both positive; and therefore, both roots will be real. And since

$$q + p^2 > p^2, \quad \text{it follows that,} \quad \sqrt{q + p^2} > p,$$

and consequently, *the roots in both these forms will have the same signs as the radicals.*

In the *first* form, the first root will be positive and the second negative, the negative root being numerically the greater.

In the *second* form, the first root is positive and the second negative, the positive root being numerically the greater.

In the third and fourth forms, if

$$p^2 > q,$$

the roots will be real, and since

$$p > \sqrt{-q + p^2},$$

they will have the same sign as the entire part of the root. Hence, *both roots will be negative in the third form, and both positive in the fourth.*

If $p^2 = q$, the quantity under the radical sign becomes 0, and the two values of $x$ in both the third and fourth forms will be equal to each other; both equal to $-p$ in the third form, and both equal to $+p$ in the fourth.

If $p^2 < q$, the quantity under the radical sign is negative, and all the roots in the third and fourth forms are imaginary.

But from the third principle demonstrated in Art. 116, the greatest value of the product of the two roots is $p^2$, and from the second principle in the same article, this product is equal to $q$; hence, the supposition of $p^2 < q$ is absurd, and the values of the roots corresponding to the supposition ought to be *impossible* or *imaginary.*

When any particular supposition gives rise to imaginary results, we interpret these results as indicating that the supposition is absurd or impossible.

17

If $p = 0$, the roots in each form become equal with contrary signs; real in the first and second forms, and imaginary in the third and fourth.

If $q = 0$, the first and third forms become the same, as also, the second and fourth.

In the former case, the first root is equal to 0, and the second root is equal to $- 2p$; in the latter case, the first root is equal to $+ 2p$, and the second to 0.

If $p = 0$ and $q = 0$, all the roots in the four forms reduce to 0.

In the preceding discussion we have made

$$p^2 > q, \quad p^2 < q, \quad \text{and} \quad p^2 = q;$$

we have also made $p$ and $q$ separately equal to 0, and then both equal to 0 at the same time.

These suppositions embrace every possible hypothesis that can be made upon $p$ and $q$.

118. The results deduced in article 117 might have been obtained by a discussion of the *four forms* themselves, instead of their roots, making use of the principles demonstrated in article 116.

In the *first* form the product of the two roots is equal to $- q$, hence the roots must have contrary signs; their sum is $- 2p$, hence the negative root is numerically the greater.

In the *second* form the product of the roots is equal to $- q$ and their sum equal to $+ 2p$; hence, their signs are unlike, and the positive root is the greater.

In the *third* form the product of the roots is equal to $+ q$; hence, their signs are alike, and their sum being equal to $- 2p$, they are both negative.

In the *fourth* form the product of the roots is equal to $+ q$, and their sum is equal to $+ 2p$; hence, their signs are alike and both positive.

If $p = 0$, the sum of the roots must be equal to 0; or the roots must be equal with contrary signs.

If $q = 0$, the product of the roots is equal to 0; hence, one of the roots must be 0, and the other will be equal to the co-efficient of the first power of the unknown quantity, taken with a contrary sign.

If $p = 0$ and $q = 0$, the sum of the roots must be equal to 0, and their product must be equal to. 0; hence, the roots themselves must both be 0.

119. There is a singular case, sometimes met with in the discussion of problems, giving rise to equations of the second degree, which needs explanation.

To discuss it, take the equation

$$ax^2 + bx = c,$$

which gives

$$x = \frac{-b \pm \sqrt{b^2 + 4ac}}{2a}.$$

If, now, we suppose $a = 0$, the expression for the value of $x$ becomes

$$x = \frac{-b \pm b}{0}, \quad \text{whence,} \quad \begin{cases} x = \dfrac{0}{0}, \\ x = -\dfrac{2b}{0} = \infty. \end{cases}$$

But the supposition $a = 0$, reduces the given equation to $bx = c$, which is an equation of the *first* degree.

The roots, found above, however, admit of interpretation.

The first one reduces to the form $\dfrac{0}{0}$ in consequence of the existence of a factor, in both numerator and denominator, which factor becomes 0 for the particular supposition. To deduce the true value of the root, in this case, take

$$x = \frac{-b + \sqrt{b^2 + 4ac}}{2a},$$

and multiply both terms of the fraction by $-b - \sqrt{b^2 + 4ac}$; after striking out the common factor $-2a$ we shall have

$$x = \frac{2c}{b + \sqrt{b^2 + 4ac}},$$

11

19

in which, if we make $a = 0$, the value of $x$ reduces to $\dfrac{c}{b}$, the same value that we should obtain by solving the simple equation $bx = c$.

The other root $\infty$, is the value towards which the expression, for the second value of $x$, continually approaches as $a$ is made smaller and smaller. It indicates that the equation, under the supposition, admits of but one root in finite terms. This should be the case, since the equation then becomes of the first degree.

120. The discussion of the following problem presents most of the circumstances usually met with in problems giving rise to equations of the second degree. In the solution of this problem, we employ the following principle of optics, viz. :—

*The intensity of a light at any given distance, is equal to its intensity at the distance 1, divided by the square of that distance.*

## Problem of the Lights.

121. Find upon the line which joins two lights, $A$ and $B$, of different intensities, the point which is equally illuminated by the lights.

Let $A$ be assumed as the origin of distances, and regard all distances measured from $A$ to the right as positive.

Let $c$ represent the distance $AB$, between the two lights ; $a$ the intensity of the light $A$ at the distance 1, and $b$, the intensity of the light $B$ at the distance 1.

Denote the distance $AC$, from $A$ to the point of equal illumination, by $x$; then will the distance from $B$ to the same point be denoted by $c - x$.

From the principle assumed in the last article, the intensity of the light $A$, at the distance 1, being $a$, its intensity at the distances 2, 3, 4, &c., will be $\dfrac{a}{4}$, $\dfrac{a}{9}$, $\dfrac{a}{16}$, &c. ; hence, at the distance $x$ it will be expressed by $\dfrac{a}{x^2}$.

20

In like manner, the intensity of $B$ at the distance $c - x$, is $\dfrac{b}{(c-x)^2}$; but, by the conditions of the problem, these two intensities are equal to each other, and therefore we have the equation

$$\frac{a}{x^2} = \frac{b}{(c-x)^2};$$

which can be put under the form

$$\frac{(c-x)^2}{x^2} = \frac{b}{a};$$

hence,

$$\frac{c-x}{x} = \frac{\pm\sqrt{b}}{\sqrt{a}}; \quad \text{whence}$$

$$x = \frac{c\sqrt{a}}{\sqrt{a}+\sqrt{b}} \quad \cdots \quad (1),$$

$$x = \frac{c\sqrt{a}}{\sqrt{a}-\sqrt{b}} \quad \cdots \quad (2).$$

Since both of these values of $x$ are always real, we conclude that there will be two points of equal illumination on the line $A B$, or on the line produced. Indeed, it is plain that there should be, not only a point of equal illumination between the lights, but also one on the prolongation of the line joining the lights and on the side of the lesser one.

To discuss these two values of $x$.

*First*, suppose $a > b$.

The first value of $x$ is positive; and since

$$\frac{\sqrt{a}}{\sqrt{a}+\sqrt{b}} < 1,$$

it will be less than $c$, and consequently, the first point $C$, will be situated between the points $A$ and $B$. We see, moreover, that the point will be nearer $B$ than $A$; for, since $a > b$, we have

$$\sqrt{a}+\sqrt{a} \quad \text{or,} \quad 2\sqrt{a} > (\sqrt{a}+\sqrt{b}), \quad \text{whence}$$

$$\frac{\sqrt{a}}{\sqrt{a}+\sqrt{b}} > \frac{1}{2}; \quad \text{and consequently,} \quad \frac{c\sqrt{a}}{\sqrt{a}+\sqrt{b}} > \frac{c}{2}.$$

The second value of $x$ is also positive; but since

$$\frac{\sqrt{a}}{\sqrt{a} - \sqrt{b}} > 1,$$

it will be greater than $c$; and consequently, the second point will be at some point $C'$, on the prolongation of $AB$, and at the right of the two lights.

This is as it should be; for, since the light at $A$ is most intense, the point of equal illumination, between the lights, ought to be nearest the light $B$; and also, the point on the prolongation of $AB$ ought to be on the side of the lesser light $B$.

*Second,* suppose $a < b$.

The first value of $x$ is positive; and since

$$\frac{\sqrt{a}}{\sqrt{a} + \sqrt{b}} < 1$$

this value of $x$ will be less than $c$; consequently, the first point will fall at some point $C$, to the right of $A$, and between $A$ and $B$.

$$\overset{\text{\tiny{$\prime$}}}{C''} \qquad \overset{\text{\tiny{$\prime$}}}{A} \qquad \overset{\text{\tiny{$\prime$}}}{C} \; \overset{\text{\tiny{$\prime$}}}{B} \qquad \overset{\text{\tiny{$\prime$}}}{C'}$$

We see, moreover, that it will be nearer $A$ than $B$; for, since $a < b$, we have

$$\sqrt{a} + \sqrt{b} > 2\sqrt{a}, \quad \text{and consequently,} \quad \frac{c\sqrt{a}}{\sqrt{a} + \sqrt{b}} < \frac{c}{2}.$$

The second value of $x$ is essentially negative, since the numerator is positive, and the denominator essentially negative.

We have agreed to consider distances from $A$ to the right positive; hence, in accordance with the rule already established for interpreting negative results, the second point of equal illumination will be found at $C''$, somewhere to the left of $A$.

This is as it should be, since, under the supposition, the light at $B$ is most intense; hence, the point of equal illumination, between the two lights, should be nearest $A$, and the point in the prolongation of $AB$, should be on the side nearest the feebler light $A$.

*Third*, suppose $a = b$, and $c > 0$.

The first value of $x$ is then positive, and equal to $\dfrac{c}{2}$ hence, the first point is midway between the two lights.

The second value of $x$ becomes $\dfrac{c\sqrt{a}}{0} = \infty$, a result which indicates that there is no other point of illumination at a finite distance from $A$.

This interpretation is evidently correct; for, under the supposition made, the lights are equally intense, and consequently, the point midway between them ought to be equally illuminated. It is also plain, that there can be no other point on the line which will enjoy that property.

*Fourth*, suppose $b = a$ and $c = 0$.

The first value of $x$ becomes, $\dfrac{0}{2\sqrt{a}} = 0$, hence the first point is at $A$.

The second value of $x$ becomes, $\dfrac{0}{0}$, a result which indicates that there are an infinite number of other points which are equally illuminated.

These conclusions are confirmed by a consideration of the conditions of the problem. Under this supposition, the lights are equal in intensity, and coincide with each other at the point $A$. That point ought then to be equally illuminated by the lights, as ought, also, every other point of the line on which the lights are placed.

*Fifth*, suppose $a > b$, or $a < b$, and $c = 0$.

Under these suppositions, both values of $x$ reduce to 0, which shows that both points of equal illumination coincide with the point $A$.

This is evidently the case, for, since $a$ is not equal to $b$, and the lights coincide at $A$, it is plain that no other point than $A$ can be equally illuminated by them.

The preceding discussion presents a striking example of the precision with which the algebraic analysis responds to all the relations which exist between the quantities that enter a problem.

### EXAMPLES INVOLVING RADICALS OF THE SECOND DEGREE.

**1.** Given, $x + \sqrt{a^2 + x^2} = \dfrac{2a^2}{\sqrt{a^2 + x^2}}$, to find the values of $x$.

By reducing to entire terms, we have,

$$x\sqrt{a^2 + x^2} + a^2 + x^2 = 2a^2,$$

by transposing, $\qquad\qquad x\sqrt{a^2 + x^2} = a^2 - x^2,$

and by squaring both members, $\quad a^2x^2 + x^4 = a^4 - 2a^2x^2 + x^4,$

whence, $\qquad\qquad\qquad\qquad\qquad 3a^2x^2 = a^4,$

and, $\qquad\qquad\qquad\qquad\qquad\qquad x = \pm\sqrt{\dfrac{a^2}{3}}.$

**2.** Given, $\sqrt{\dfrac{a^2}{x^2} + b^2} - \sqrt{\dfrac{a^2}{x^2} - b^2} = b$, to find the values of $x$.

By transposing, $\quad \sqrt{\dfrac{a^2}{x^2} + b^2} = \sqrt{\dfrac{a^2}{x^2} - b^2} + b\,;$

squaring both members, $\dfrac{a^2}{x^2} + b^2 = \dfrac{a^2}{x^2} - b^2 + 2b\sqrt{\dfrac{a^2}{x^2} - b^2} + b^2\,;$

whence, $\quad b^2 = 2b\sqrt{\dfrac{a^2}{x^2} - b^2},\quad$ and $\quad b = 2\sqrt{\dfrac{a^2}{x^2} - b^2}\,;$

squaring both members, $\qquad b^2 = \dfrac{4a^2}{x^2} - 4b^2\,;$

and hence, $\qquad\qquad x^2 = \dfrac{4a^2}{5b^2},\quad$ and $\quad x = \pm\dfrac{2a}{b\sqrt{5}}.$

**3.** Given, $\dfrac{a}{x} + \sqrt{\dfrac{a^2 - x^2}{x^2}} = \dfrac{x}{b}$, to find the values of $x$.

$$\textit{Ans. } x = \pm\sqrt{2ab - b^2}.$$

**4.** Given, $\sqrt{\dfrac{x + a}{x}} + 2\sqrt{\dfrac{a}{x + a}} = b^2\sqrt{\dfrac{x}{x + a}}$, to find the values of $x$.

$$\textit{Ans. } x = \dfrac{a}{(b \mp 1)^2}.$$

24

5. Given, $\dfrac{a - \sqrt{a^2 - x^2}}{a + \sqrt{a^2 - x^2}} = b$, to find the values of $x$.

$$Ans. \quad x = \pm \frac{2a\sqrt{b}}{1 + b}.$$

6. Given, $\dfrac{\sqrt{x} + \sqrt{x - a}}{\sqrt{x} - \sqrt{x - a}} = \dfrac{n^2 a}{x - a}$, to find the values of $x$.

$$Ans. \quad x = \frac{a(1 \pm n)^2}{1 \pm 2n}.$$

7. Given, $\dfrac{\sqrt{a + x}}{\sqrt{x}} + \dfrac{\sqrt{a - x}}{\sqrt{x}} = \sqrt{\dfrac{x}{b}}$, to find the values of $x$.

$$Ans. \quad x = \pm 2\sqrt{ab - b^2}.$$

8. Given, $\dfrac{a + x + \sqrt{2ax + x^2}}{a + x} = b$, to find the values of $x$.

$$Ans. \quad x = \frac{\pm a(1 \pm \sqrt{2b - b^2})}{\sqrt{2b - b^2}}.$$

## Of Trinomial Equations.

**122.** A *trinomial equation* is one which involves only terms containing two different powers of the unknown quantity and a known term or terms.

**123.** Every trinomial equation can be reduced to the form

$$x^m + 2px^n = q \quad \cdots \cdots \quad (1),$$

in which $m$ and $n$ are positive whole numbers, and $p$ and $q$ known quantities, by means of a rule entirely similar to that given in article 111.

If we suppose $m = 2$ and $n = 1$, equation (1) becomes

$$x^2 + 2px = q,$$

a trinomial equation of the second degree.

**124.** The solution of trinomial equations of the second degree, has already been explained. The methods, there explained, are, with some slight modifications, applicable to all trinomial equations in which $m = 2n$, that is, to all equations of the form

$$x^{2n} + 2px^n = q.$$

25

To demonstrate a rule for the solution of equations of this form, let us place

$$x^n = y; \quad \text{whence,} \quad x^{2n} = y^2.$$

These values of $x^n$ and $x^{2n}$, being substituted in the given equation, reduce it to

$$y^2 + 2py = q,$$

whence, $$y = -p \pm \sqrt{q + p^2},$$

or, $$x^n = -p \pm \sqrt{q + p^2}.$$

Now, the $n^{th}$ root, of the first member, is $x$ (Art. 18), and although we have not yet explained how to extract the $n^{th}$ root of an algebraic quantity, we may indicate the $n^{th}$ root of the second member. Hence, (axiom 6),

$$x = \sqrt[n]{-p \pm \sqrt{q + p^2}}.$$

Hence, to solve a trinomial equation which can be reduced to the form $x^{2n} + 2px^n = q$, we have the following

## RULE.

*Reduce the equation to the form of $x^{2n} + 2px^n = q$; the values of the unknown quantity will then be found by extracting the $n^{th}$ root of half the co-efficient of the lowest power of the unknown quantity with its sign changed, plus or minus the square root of the second member increased by the square of half the co-efficient of the lowest power of the unknown quantity.*

If $n = 2$, the roots of the equation are of the form

$$x = \pm \sqrt{-p \pm \sqrt{q + p^2}}.$$

We see that the unknown quantity has four values, since each of the signs $+$ and $-$, which affect the first radical can be combined, in succession, with each of the signs which affect the second; but *these values, taken two and two, are numerically equal, and have contrary signs.*

## EXAMPLES.

1. Take the equation
$$x^4 - 25x^2 = -144.$$

This being of the required form, we have by application of the rule,
$$x = \pm \sqrt{\frac{25}{2} \pm \sqrt{-144 + \frac{625}{4}}},$$

whence, $\qquad x = \pm \sqrt{\frac{25}{2} \pm \frac{7}{2}};$

hence, the four roots are $+4$, $-4$, $+3$, and $-3$.

2. As a second example, take the equation
$$x^4 - 7x^2 = 8.$$

Whence, by the rule,
$$x = \pm \sqrt{\frac{7}{2} \pm \sqrt{8 + \frac{49}{4}}} = \pm \sqrt{\frac{7}{2} \pm \frac{9}{2}};$$

hence, the four roots are,
$$+2\sqrt{2}, \quad -2\sqrt{2}, \quad +\sqrt{-1} \quad \text{and} \quad -\sqrt{-1};$$
the last two are imaginary.

3. $x^4 - (2bc + 4a^2) x^2 = -b^2c^2.$

$\qquad\qquad Ans. \ x = \pm \sqrt{bc + 2a^2 \pm 2a\sqrt{bc + a^2}}.$

4. $2x - 7\sqrt{x} = 99.$ $\qquad\qquad Ans. \ x = 81, \ x = \dfrac{121}{4}.$

5. $\dfrac{a}{b} - bx^4 + \dfrac{c}{d}x^2 = 0.$ $\quad Ans. \ x = \pm \sqrt{\dfrac{c \pm \sqrt{4ad^2 + c^2}}{2bd}}.$

125. The solution of trinomial equations of the fourth degree requires the extraction of the square root of expressions of the form of $a \pm \sqrt{b}$ in which $a$ and $b$ are positive or negative, numerical or algebraic. The expression $\sqrt{a \pm \sqrt{b}}$ can sometimes be reduced to the form of $a' \pm \sqrt{b'}$ or to the form $\sqrt{a''} \pm \sqrt{b''}$; and when such transformation is possible, it is

advantageous to effect it, since, in this case, we have only to extract two simple square roots; whereas, the expression

$$\sqrt{a \pm \sqrt{b}},$$

requires the extraction of the square root of the square root.

To deduce formulas for making the required transformation, let us assume

$$p + q = \sqrt{a + \sqrt{b}} \quad \cdots \quad (1),$$

$$p - q = \sqrt{a - \sqrt{b}} \quad \cdots \quad (2);$$

in which $p$ and $q$ are arbitrary quantities.

It is now required to find such values for $p$ and $q$ as will satisfy equations (1) and (2).

By squaring both members of equations (1) and (2), we have

$$p^2 + 2pq + q^2 = a + \sqrt{b} \cdots \quad (3),$$

$$p^2 - 2pq + q^2 = a - \sqrt{b} \cdots \quad (4).$$

Adding equations (3) and (4), member to member, we get

$$p^2 + q^2 = a \cdots \quad (5).$$

Multiplying (1) and (2), member by member, we have,

$$p^2 - q^2 = \sqrt{a^2 - b}.$$

Let us now represent $\sqrt{a^2 - b}$ by $c$. Substituting in the last equation,

$$p^2 - q^2 = c \cdots \quad (6).$$

From (5) and (6) we readily deduce,

$$p = \pm \sqrt{\frac{a + c}{2}} \quad \text{and} \quad q = \pm \sqrt{\frac{a - c}{2}};$$

these values substituted for $p$ and $q$, in equations (1) and (2), give

$$\sqrt{a + \sqrt{b}} = \pm \sqrt{\frac{a + c}{2}} \pm \sqrt{\frac{a - c}{2}};$$

$$\sqrt{a - \sqrt{b}} = \pm \sqrt{\frac{a + c}{2}} \mp \sqrt{\frac{a - c}{2}};$$

hence,

$$\sqrt{a + \sqrt{b}} = \pm \left( \sqrt{\frac{a+c}{2}} + \sqrt{\frac{a-c}{2}} \right) \quad \cdot \quad (7),$$

and

$$\sqrt{a - \sqrt{b}} = \pm \left( \sqrt{\frac{a+c}{2}} - \sqrt{\frac{a-c}{2}} \right) \quad \cdot \quad (8).$$

Now, if $a^2 - b$ is a perfect square, its square root, $c$, will be a rational quantity, and the application of one of the formulas (7) or (8) will reduce the given expression to the required form. If $a^2 - b$ is not a perfect square, the application of the formulas will not simplify the given expression, for, we shall still have to extract the square root of a square root.

Therefore, in general, this transformation is not used, unless $a^2 - b$ is a perfect square.

### EXAMPLES.

1. Reduce $\sqrt{94 + 42\sqrt{5}} = \sqrt{94 + \sqrt{8820}}$, to its simplest form. We have, $a = 94$, $b = 8820$,

whence, $c = \sqrt{a^2 - b} = \sqrt{8836 - 8820} = 4$,

a rational quantity; formula (7) is therefore applicable to this case, and we have

$$\sqrt{94 + 42\sqrt{5}} = \pm \left( \sqrt{\frac{94+4}{2}} + \sqrt{\frac{94-4}{2}} \right),$$

or, reducing, $= \pm (\sqrt{49} + \sqrt{45})$;

hence, $\sqrt{94 + 42\sqrt{5}} = \pm (7 + 3\sqrt{5})$.

This may be verified; for,

$$(7 + 3\sqrt{5})^2 = 49 + 45 + 42\sqrt{5} = 94 + 42\sqrt{5}.$$

2. Reduce $\sqrt{np + 2m^2 - 2m\sqrt{np + m^2}}$, to its simplest form. We have

$$a = np + 2m^2, \quad \text{and} \quad b = 4m^2(np + m^2),$$
$$a^2 - b = n^2p^2, \quad \text{and} \quad c = \sqrt{a^2 - b} = np;$$

29

and therefore, formula (7) is applicable. It gives,

$$\pm \left( \sqrt{\frac{np + 2m^2 + np}{2}} - \sqrt{\frac{np + 2m^2 - np}{2}} \right),$$

and, reducing, $\qquad \pm (\sqrt{np + m^2} - m).$

3. Reduce to its simplest form,

$$\sqrt{16 + 30\sqrt{-1}} + \sqrt{16 - 30\sqrt{-1}}.$$

By applying the formulas, we find

$$\sqrt{16 + 30\sqrt{-1}} = 5 + 3\sqrt{-1},$$

and $\qquad \sqrt{16 - 30\sqrt{-1}} = 5 - 3\sqrt{-1} :$

hence, $\qquad \sqrt{16 + 30\sqrt{-1}} + \sqrt{16 - 30\sqrt{-1}} = 10.$

This example shows that the transformation is applicable to imaginary expressions.

4. Reduce to its simplest form,

$$\sqrt{28 + 10\sqrt{3}}. \qquad\qquad Ans. \ \ 5 + \sqrt{3}.$$

5. Reduce to its simplest form,

$$\sqrt{1 + 4\sqrt{-3}}. \qquad\qquad Ans. \ \ 2 + \sqrt{-3}.$$

6. Reduce to its simplest form,

$$\sqrt{bc + 2b\sqrt{bc - b^2}} - \sqrt{bc - 2b\sqrt{bc - b^2}}.$$

$$Ans. \ \ \pm 2b.$$

7. Reduce to its simplest form,

$$\sqrt{ab + 4c^2 - d^2 - 2\sqrt{4abc^2 - abd^2}}.$$

$$Ans. \ \ \sqrt{ab} - \sqrt{4c^2 - d^2}.$$

EQUATIONS OF THE SECOND DEGREE.

*Equations of the Second Degree involving two or more unknown quantities.*

**126.** Every equation of the second degree, containing two unknown quantities, is of the general form

$$ay^2 + bxy + cx^2 + dy + fx + g = 0;$$

or a particular case of that form. For, this equation contains terms involving the squares of both unknown quantities, their product, their first powers, and a known term.

In order to discuss, generally, equations of the second degree involving two unknown quantities, let us take the two equations of the most general form

$$a y^2 + b xy + c x^2 + d y + f x + g = 0,$$

and

$$a'y^2 + b'xy + c'x^2 + d'y + f'x + g' = 0.$$

Arranging them with reference to $x$, they become

$$c x^2 + (b y + f)x + a y^2 + d y + g = 0,$$
$$c'x^2 + (b'y + f')x + a'y^2 + d'y + g' = 0;$$

from which we may eliminate $x^2$, after having made its co-efficient the same in both equations.

By multiplying both members of the first equation by $c'$, and both members of the second by $c$, they become,

$$cc'x^2 + (b y + f)c'x + (a y^2 + d y + g)c' = 0,$$
$$cc'x^2 + (b'y + f')c x + (a'y^2 + d'y + g')c = 0.$$

Subtracting one from the other, member from member, we have

$$[(bc' - cb')y + fc' - cf']x + (ac' - ca')y^2 + (dc' - cd')y + gc' - cg' = 0,$$

which gives

$$x = \frac{(ca' - ac')y^2 + (cd' - dc')y + cg' - gc'}{(bc' - cb')y + fc' - cf'}.$$

This value being substituted for $x$ in one of the proposed equations, will give *a final equation*, involving only $y$.

But without effecting the substitution, which would lead to a very complicated result, it is easy to perceive that the final equation involving $y$, will be of the fourth degree. For, the

31

numerator of the value of $x$ being of the form
$$my^2 + ny + p,$$
its square will be of the fourth degree, and this square forms one of the parts in the result of the substitution.

Therefore, in general, *the solution of two equations of the second degree, involving two unknown quantities, depends upon that of an equation of the fourth degree, involving one unknown quantity.*

**127.** Since we have not yet explained the manner of solving equations of the fourth degree, it follows that we cannot, as yet, solve the general case of two equations of the second degree involving two unknown quantities. There are, however, some particular cases that admit of solution, by the application of the rules already demonstrated.

*First.* We can always solve two equations containing two unknown quantities, when one of the equations is of the second degree, and the other of the first.

For, we can find the value of one of the unknown quantities in terms of the other and known quantities, from the latter equation, and by substituting this in the former, we shall have a single equation of the second degree containing but one unknown quantity, which can be solved.

Thus, if we have the two equations
$$x^2 + 2y^2 = 22 \ \cdot \ \cdot \ \cdot \ \cdot \ (1),$$
$$2x - y = 1 \ \cdot \ \cdot \ \cdot \ \cdot \ (2),$$
we can find from equation (2),
$$x = \frac{1+y}{2}; \quad \text{whence,} \quad x^2 = \frac{1 + 2y + y^2}{4};$$
and by substituting this expression for $x^2$ in equation (1), we find
$$\frac{1 + 2y + y^2}{4} + 2y^2 = 22;$$
whence we get the values of $y$: that is,
$$y = 3 \quad \text{and} \quad y = -\frac{29}{9};$$
and by substituting in equation (2) we find,
$$x = 2 \quad \text{and} \quad x = -\frac{10}{9}.$$

*Second.* We can always solve two equations of the second degree containing two unknown quantities when they are both homogeneous with respect to these quantities.

For, we can substitute for one of the unknown quantities, an auxiliary unknown quantity multiplied into the second unknown quantity, and by combining the two resulting equations we can find an equation of the second degree, from which the value of the auxiliary unknown quantity may be determined, and thence the values of the required quantities can easily be found.

Take, for example, the equations

$$x^2 + xy - y^2 = 5 \quad \cdots \quad (1),$$
$$3x^2 - 2xy - 2y^2 = 6 \quad \cdots \quad (2).$$

Substitute for $y$, $px$, $p$ being unknown, the given equations become

$$x^2 + px^2 - p^2x^2 = 5 \quad \cdots \quad (3),$$
$$3x^2 - 2px^2 - 2p^2x^2 = 6 \quad \cdots \quad (4).$$

Finding the values of $x^2$ in terms of $p$, from equations (3) and (4), and placing them equal to each other, we deduce

$$\frac{5}{1 + p - p^2} = \frac{6}{3 - 2p - 2p^2};$$

or reducing, $\qquad p^2 + 4p = \dfrac{9}{4};$

whence, $\qquad p = \dfrac{1}{2}, \quad \text{and} \quad p = -\dfrac{9}{2}.$

Considering the positive value of $p$, we have, by substituting it in equation (3),

$$x^2 \left(1 + \frac{1}{2} - \frac{1}{4}\right) = 5,$$

or, $\qquad x^2 = 4;$

whence, $\qquad x = 2 \quad \text{and} \quad x = -2:$

and since $y = px$ we have $y = 1$ and $y = -1.$

*Third.* There are certain other cases which admit of solution, but for which no fixed rule can be given.

We shall illustrate the manner of treating these cases, by the solution of the following

1. Given, $\left.\begin{array}{c} \dfrac{xy}{\sqrt{\dfrac{x}{y}}} = 48, \\[3em] \dfrac{xy}{\sqrt{\dfrac{x}{x}}} = 24, \end{array}\right\}$ to find the values of $x$ and $y$.

Dividing the first by the second, member by member, we have

$$\frac{\sqrt{x}}{\sqrt{\dfrac{x}{y}}} = 2, \quad \text{or} \quad \sqrt{y} = 2; \quad \text{whence} \quad y = 4;$$

and by substituting in the second equation, we get

$$\sqrt{x} = 6, \quad \text{and} \quad x = 36.$$

2. Given, $\left.\begin{array}{l} x + \sqrt{xy} + y = 19, \\ x^2 + xy + y^2 = 133, \end{array}\right\}$ to find the values of $x$ and $y$.

Dividing the second by the first, member by member, we have

$$x - \sqrt{xy} + y = 7.$$

But, $\qquad\qquad x + \sqrt{xy} + y = 19:$

adding these, member to member, and dividing by 2, we find

$$x + y = 13,$$

which substituted in the first equation, gives,

$$\sqrt{xy} = 6, \quad \text{or} \quad xy = 36, \quad \text{and} \quad x = \frac{36}{y}.$$

Substituting this expression for $x$, in the preceding equation, we get,

$$\frac{36}{y} + y = 13,$$

or, $\qquad\qquad y^2 - 13y = -36;$

whence, $\qquad y = \dfrac{13}{2} \pm \sqrt{-36 + \dfrac{169}{4}} = \dfrac{13}{2} \pm \dfrac{5}{2}:$

and finally, $\qquad y = 9, \quad \text{or} \quad y = 4;$

and since $\qquad x + y = 13,$

$$x = 4, \quad \text{or} \quad x = 9.$$

3. Find the values of $x$ and $y$, in the equations

$$x^2 + 3x + y = 73 - 2xy$$
$$y^2 + 3y + x = 44.$$

By transposition, the first equation becomes,

$$x^2 + 2xy + 3x + y = 73;$$

to which, if the second be added, member to member, there results,

$$x^2 + 2xy + y^2 + 4x + 4y = (x + y)^2 + 4(x + y) = 117.$$

If, now, in the equation

$$(x + y)^2 + 4(x + y) = 117,$$

we regard $x + y$ as a single unknown quantity, we shall have

$$x + y = -2 \pm \sqrt{117 + 4};$$

hence,  $x + y = -2 + 11 = 9,$

and  $x + y = -2 - 11 = -13;$

whence,  $x = 9 - y,$  and  $x = -13 - y.$

Substituting these values of $x$ in the second equation, we have

$$y^2 + 2y = 35, \quad \text{for} \quad x = 9 - y,$$

and  $y^2 + 2y = 57,$  for  $x = -13 - y.$

The first equation gives,

$$y = 5, \quad \text{and} \quad y = -7,$$

and the second,

$$y = -1 + \sqrt{58}, \quad \text{and} \quad y = -1 - \sqrt{58}.$$

The corresponding values of $x$, are

$$x = 4, \qquad x = 16;$$
$$x = -12 - \sqrt{58}, \quad \text{and} \quad x = -12 + \sqrt{58}.$$

4. Find the values of $x$ and $y$, in the equations

$$x^2y^2 + xy^2 + xy = 600 - (y + 2)x^2y^3$$
$$x + y^2 = 14 - y.$$

From the first equation, we have

$$x^2y^2 + (y^2 + 2y)x^2y^2 + xy^2 + xy = 600,$$

or,  $x^2y^2(1 + y^2 + 2y) + xy(1 + y) = 600,$

or, again,  $x^2y^2(1 + y)^2 + xy(1 + y) = 600;$

which is of the form of an equation of the second degree, re-
garding $xy(1+y)$ as the unknown quantity. Hence,

$$xy\,(1+y) = -\tfrac{1}{2} \pm \sqrt{600 + \tfrac{1}{4}} = -\tfrac{1}{2} \pm \sqrt{\frac{2401}{4}}\,;$$

and if we discuss only the roots which belong to the $+$ value
of the radical, we have

$$xy\,(1+y) = -\frac{1}{2} + \frac{49}{2} = 24\,;$$

and hence, $$x = \frac{24}{y + y^2}.$$

Substituting this value for $x$ in the second equation, we have

$$(y^2 + y)^2 - 14\,(y^2 + y) = -24\,;$$

whence, $\quad y^2 + y = 12, \quad$ and $\quad y^2 + y = 2.$

From the first equation, we have

$$y = -\frac{1}{2} \pm \frac{7}{2} = 3, \quad \text{or} \quad -4\,;$$

and the corresponding values of $x$, from the equation

$$x = \frac{24}{y^2 + y} = 2.$$

From the second equation, we have

$$y = 1, \quad \text{and} \quad y = -2\,;$$

which gives $$x = 12.$$

5. Given, $\quad x^2y + xy^2 = 6, \quad$ and $\quad x^3y^2 + x^2y^3 = 12, \quad$ to find the
values of $x$ and $y$.

$$\textit{Ans.} \quad \begin{cases} x = 2 \text{ or } 1, \\ y = 1 \text{ or } 2. \end{cases}$$

6. Given, $\quad \begin{cases} x^2 + x + y = 18 - y^2 \\ xy = 6 \end{cases}$ to find the values of $x$ and $y$.

$$\textit{Ans.} \quad \begin{cases} x = 3, \text{ or } 2; \text{ or } -3 \pm \sqrt{3}, \\ y = 2, \text{ or } 3; \text{ or } -3 \mp \sqrt{3}. \end{cases}$$

*Problems giving rise to Equations of the Second Degree con-
taining two or more unknown quantities.*

1. Find two numbers such, that the sum of the respective
products of the first multiplied by $a$, and the second multiplied
by $b$, shall be equal to $2s$; and the product of the one by
the other equal to $p$.

Let $x$ and $y$ denote the required numbers, and we have

$$ax + by = 2s,$$

and $$xy = p.$$

From the first

$$y = \frac{2s - ax}{b};$$

whence, by substituting in the second, and reducing,

$$ax^2 - 2sx = -bp.$$

Therefore, $$x = \frac{s}{a} \pm \frac{1}{a}\sqrt{s^2 - abp},$$

and consequently, $$y = \frac{s}{b} \mp \frac{1}{b}\sqrt{s^2 - abp}.$$

Let $a = b = 1$; the values of $x$, and $y$, then reduce to

$$x = s \pm \sqrt{s^2 - p}, \quad \text{and} \quad y = s \mp \sqrt{s^2 - p};$$

whence we see that, under this supposition, the two values of $x$ are equal to those of $y$, taken in an inverse order; which shows, that if

$$s + \sqrt{s^2 - p} \quad \text{represents the value of } x, \quad s - \sqrt{s^2 - p}$$

will represent the corresponding value of $y$, and conversely.

This relation is explained by observing that, under the last supposition, the given equations become

$$x + y = 2s, \quad \text{and} \quad xy = p;$$

and the question is then reduced to *finding two numbers of which the sum is 2s, and their product p;* or in other words, *to divide a number 2s, into two such parts, that their product may be equal to a given number p.*

2. To find four numbers, such that the sum of the first and fourth shall be equal to $2s$, the sum of the second and third equal to $2s'$, the sum of their squares equal to $4c^2$, and the product of the first and fourth equal to the product of the second and third.

Let $u$, $x$, $y$, and $z$, denote the numbers, respectively. Then, from the conditions of the problem, we shall have

$$u + z = 2s \quad \text{1st condition;}$$
$$x + y = 2s' \quad \text{2d} \quad \text{``}$$
$$u^2 + x^2 + y^2 + z^2 = 4c^2 \quad \text{3d} \quad \text{``}$$
$$uz = xy \quad \text{4th} \quad \text{``}$$

At first sight, it may appear difficult to find the values of the unknown quantities, but by the aid of an *auxiliary unknown quantity*, they are easily determined.

Let $p$ be the unknown product of the 1st and 4th, or 2d and 3d; we shall then have

$$\left\{ \begin{aligned} u + z &= 2s, \\ uz &= p, \end{aligned} \right\} \quad \text{which give,} \quad \left\{ \begin{aligned} u &= s + \sqrt{s^2 - p}, \\ z &= s - \sqrt{s^2 - p}. \end{aligned} \right.$$

and

$$\left\{ \begin{aligned} x + y &= 2s', \\ xy &= p, \end{aligned} \right\} \quad \text{which give,} \quad \left\{ \begin{aligned} x &= s' + \sqrt{s'^2 - p}, \\ y &= s' - \sqrt{s'^2 - p}. \end{aligned} \right.$$

Now, by substituting these values of $u$, $x$, $y$, $z$, in the third equation of the problem, it becomes

$$(s + \sqrt{s^2 - p})^2 + (s - \sqrt{s^2 - p})^2 + (s' + \sqrt{s'^2 - p})^2$$
$$+ (s' - \sqrt{s'^2 - p})^2 = 4c^2;$$

and by developing and reducing,

$$4s^2 + 4s'^2 - 4p = 4c^2: \quad \text{hence,} \quad p = s^2 + s'^2 - c^2.$$

Substituting this value for $p$, in the expressions for $u$, $x$, $y$, $z$, we find

$$\left\{ \begin{aligned} u &= s + \sqrt{c^2 - s'^2}, \\ z &= s - \sqrt{c^2 - s'^2}, \end{aligned} \right. \qquad \left\{ \begin{aligned} x &= s' + \sqrt{c^2 - s^2}, \\ y &= s' - \sqrt{c^2 - s^2}. \end{aligned} \right.$$

These values evidently satisfy the last equation of the problem; for

$$uz = (s + \sqrt{c^2 - s'^2})(s - \sqrt{c^2 - s'^2}) = s^2 - c^2 + s'^2,$$
$$xy = (s' + \sqrt{c^2 - s^2})(s' - \sqrt{c^2 - s^2}) = s'^2 - c^2 + s^2.$$

REMARK.—This problem shows how much the introduction of an *unknown auxiliary* often facilitates the determination of the principal unknown quantities. There are other problems of the same kind, which lead to equations of a degree superior to the second, and yet they may be resolved by the aid of equations of the first and second degrees, by introducing *unknown auxiliaries.*

3. Given the sum of two numbers equal to $a$, and the sum of their cubes equal to $c$, to find the numbers

By the conditions
$$\begin{cases} x + y = a \\ x^3 + y^3 = c. \end{cases}$$

Putting $x = s + z$, and $y = s - z$, we have $a = 2s$,

and
$$\begin{cases} x^3 = s^3 + 3s^2z + 3sz^2 + z^3 \\ y^3 = s^3 - 3s^2z + 3sz^2 - z^3 : \end{cases}$$

hence, by addition, $\quad x^3 + y^3 = 2s^3 + 6sz^2 = c;$

whence, $\qquad z^2 = \dfrac{c - 2s^3}{6s}, \quad$ and $\quad z = \pm\sqrt{\dfrac{c - 2s^3}{6s}},$

or, $\qquad x = s \pm\sqrt{\dfrac{c - 2s^3}{6s}}, \quad$ and $\quad y = s \mp\sqrt{\dfrac{c - 2s^3}{6s}} \; ;$

and by substituting for $s$ its value,

$$x = \frac{a}{2} \pm\sqrt{\left(\frac{c - \frac{1}{4}a^3}{3a}\right)} = \frac{a}{2} \pm\sqrt{\frac{4c - a^3}{12a}},$$

and $\qquad y = \dfrac{a}{2} \mp\sqrt{\left(\dfrac{c - \frac{1}{4}a^3}{3a}\right)} = \dfrac{a}{2} \mp\sqrt{\dfrac{4c - a^3}{12a}}.$

4. The sum of the squares of two numbers is expressed by $a$, and the difference of their squares by $b$: what are the numbers?

$$Ans. \; \sqrt{\frac{a + b}{2}}, \; \sqrt{\frac{a - b}{2}}.$$

5. What three numbers are they, which, multiplied two and two, and each product divided by the third number, give the quotients, $a$, $b$, $c$?

$$Ans. \; \sqrt{ab}, \; \sqrt{ac}, \; \sqrt{bc}.$$

6. The sum of two numbers is 8, and the sum of their cubes is 152: what are the numbers?    *Ans.* 3 and 5.

7. Find two numbers, whose difference added to the difference of their squares is 150, and whose sum added to the sum of their squares, is 330.    *Ans.* 9 and 15.

8. There are two numbers whose difference is 15, and half their product is equal to the cube of the lesser number: what are the numbers?    *Ans.* 3 and 18.

9. What two numbers are those whose sum multiplied by the greater, is equal to 77; and whose difference, multiplied by the lesser, is equal to 12?

*Ans.* 4 and 7, or $\frac{3}{2}\sqrt{2}$ and $\frac{11}{2}\sqrt{2}$.

10. Divide 100 into two such parts, that the sum of their square roots may be 14.    *Ans.* 64 and 36.

11. It is required to divide the number 24 into two such parts, that their product may be equal to 35 times their difference.    *Ans.* 10 and 14.

12. What two numbers are they, whose product is 255, and the sum of whose squares is 514?    *Ans.* 15 and 17.

13. There is a number expressed by two digits, which, when divided by the sum of the digits, gives a quotient greater by 2 than the first digit; but if the digits be inverted, and the resulting number be divided by a number greater by 1 than the sum of the digits, the quotient will exceed the former quotient by 2: what is the number?    *Ans.* 24.

14. A regiment, in garrison, consisting of a certain number of companies, receives orders to send 216 men on duty, each company to furnish an equal number. Before the order was executed, three of the companies were sent on another service, and it was then found that each company that remained would have to send 12 men additional, in order to make up the complement, 216. How many companies were in the regiment, and what number of men did each of the remaining companies send?

*Ans.* 9 companies: each that remained sent 36 men.

15. Find three numbers such, that their sum shall be 14, the sum of their squares equal to 84, and the product of the first and third equal to the square of the second.

Ans. 2, 4 and 8.

16. It is required to find a number, expressed by three digits, such, that the sum of the squares of the digits shall be 104; the square of the middle digit to exceed twice the product of the other two by 4; and if 594 be subtracted from the number, the remainder will be expressed by the same figures, but with the extreme digits reversed. Ans. 862.

17. A person has three kinds of goods which together cost $230$\frac{5}{24}$. A pound of each article costs as many $\frac{1}{24}$ dollars as there are pounds in that article: he has one-third more of the second than of the first, and $3\frac{1}{2}$ times as much of the third as of the second : How many pounds has he of each article?

Ans. 15 of the 1st, 20 of the 2d, 70 of the 3d.

18. Two merchants each sold the same kind of stuff : the second sold 3 yards more of it than the first, and together, they received 35 dollars. The first said to the second, " I would have received 24 dollars for your stuff." The other replied, " And I would have received $12\frac{1}{2}$ dollars for yours." How many yards did each of them sell?

Ans. $\begin{Bmatrix} \text{1st merchant} & 15 \\ \text{2d} & - & - & - & 18 \end{Bmatrix}$ or $\begin{Bmatrix} 5 \\ 8. \end{Bmatrix}$

19. A widow possessed 13000 dollars, which she divided into two parts, and placed them at interest, in such a manner, that the incomes from them were equal. If she had put out the first portion at the same rate as the second, she would have drawn for this part 360 dollars interest; and if she had placed the second out at the same rate as the first, she would have drawn for it 490 dollars interest. What were the two rates of interest?

Ans. 7 and 6 per cent.

41

142. THE general form of the equation of the second degree in a plane is

$$A x^2 + B x y + C y^2 + D x + E y + M = 0, \quad (199)$$

and that of the equation in space is

$$A x^2 + B x y + C y^2 + D x z + E y z + F z^2$$
$$+ H x + I y + K z + M = 0. \quad (200)$$

143. *Problem.* To reduce the general equation of the second degree in a plane to its simplest form.

*Solution.* I. By substituting in (199) equations (18) and (19) for transformation from one system of rectangular co-ordinates to another, the origin being the same ; representing the coefficients of $x_1^2$, $y_1^2$, $x_1$, and $y_1$ by $A_1$, $B_1$, $D_1$, and $E_1$; and taking $\alpha$ of such a value that the coefficient of $x_1 y_1$ may be zero ; (199) becomes

$$A_1 x_1^2 + B_1 y_1^2 + D_1 x_1 + E_1 y_1 + M = 0. \quad (201)$$

in which we have

$$A_1 = A \cos^2 \alpha + B \sin. \alpha \cos. \alpha + C \sin^2 \alpha \quad (202)$$

$$B_1 = A \sin^2 \alpha - B \sin. \alpha \cos. \alpha + C \cos^2 \alpha \quad (203)$$

$$D_1 = D \cos. \alpha + E \sin. \alpha \quad (204)$$

$$E_1 = - D \sin. \alpha + E \cos. \alpha, \quad (205)$$

and $\alpha$ satisfies the equation

$$2\,(C-A)\sin.\,\alpha\cos.\,\alpha + B\,(\cos.^2\alpha - \sin.^2\alpha) = 0. \quad (206)$$

II. If, now, we substitute the formulas (20) for transposing the origin in (201); using $x_2$ and $y_2$ for the new coördinates; take the coördinates $a$ and $b$ of the new origin of such values, that the coefficients of $x_2$ and $y_2$ may be zero; and denote the sum of the terms which do not contain $x_2$ or $y_2$ by $M_1$; (201) becomes

$$A_1\,x_2^2 + B_1\,y_2^2 + M_1 = 0, \quad (207)$$

in which

$$M_1 = A_1\,a^2 + B_1\,b^2 + D_1\,a + E_1\,b + M, \quad (208)$$

and $a$ and $b$ satisfy the equations

$$2\,A_1\,a + D_1 = 0 \quad (209)$$

$$2\,B_1\,b + E_1 = 0. \quad (210)$$

The form (207), to which the given equation is thus reduced, is its simplest form.

144. *Corollary.* If we take $L$, $L'$ such that

$$L = 2\,A\cos.\,\alpha + B\sin.\,\alpha \quad (211)$$

$$L' = 2\,C\sin.\,\alpha + B\cos.\,\alpha, \quad (212)$$

these values substituted in (206), and the double of (202) give

$$2\,A_1 = L\cos.\,\alpha + L'\sin.\,\alpha \quad (213)$$

$$0 = L'\cos.\,\alpha - L\sin.\,\alpha. \quad (214)$$

The product of (213) by cos. $\alpha$, diminished by that of (214) by sin. $\alpha$, reduced by means of the equation

$$\sin.^2\alpha + \cos.^2\alpha = 1 \quad (215)$$

43

is, by (211),

$$2 A_1 \cos. \alpha = L = 2 A \cos. \alpha + B \sin. \alpha, \qquad (216)$$

or
$$2 (A_1 - A) \cos. \alpha - B \sin. \alpha = 0. \qquad (217)$$

The product of (213) by sin. $\alpha$ added to that of (214) by cos. $\alpha$ is, by (215) and (212),

$$2 A_1 \sin. \alpha = L' = 2 C \sin. \alpha + B \cos. \alpha \qquad (218)$$

$$2 (A_1 - C) \sin. \alpha - B \cos. \alpha = 0. \qquad (219)$$

The product of (217) by $2 (A_1 - C)$ added to that of (219) by $B$ is, when divided by cos. $\alpha$,

$$4 (A_1 - A) (A_1 - C) - B^2 = 0, \qquad (220)$$

from which equation the value of $A_1$ may be determined, that is, if we put $X$ instead of $A^1$, $A_1$ *is a root of the quadratic equation*

$$4 (X - A) (X - C) - B^2 = 0; \qquad (221)$$

the roots of which are

$$X = \tfrac{1}{2}(A + C) \pm \tfrac{1}{2}\sqrt{(B^2 + A^2 - 2 A C + C^2)}$$
$$= \tfrac{1}{2}(A + C) \pm \tfrac{1}{2}\sqrt{[B^2 + (A - C)^2]}. \qquad (222)$$

**145. Corollary.** If we take $L_1$ and $L'_1$ such that

$$L_1 = 2 A \sin. \alpha - B \cos. \alpha \qquad (223)$$
$$L'_1 = 2 C \cos. \alpha - B \sin. \alpha, \qquad (224)$$

we find that by changing $A$ to $C$, $C$ to $A$ and $B$ to $-B$, $A_1$ (202) becomes $B_1$ (203), 206 remains unchanged except in the reversal of its sign, $L$ (211) becomes $L'_1$ (224) and $L'$

---
Inclination of axis.
---

(212) becomes $L_1$ (223). But, by the same changes, (220) becomes

$$4\,(B_1 - C)\,(B_1 - A) - B^2 = 0, \qquad (225)$$

so that $B_1$ is determined by precisely the same equation with which $A_1$ is determined in (220), and is a root of the equation (221).

The sum of the roots of the equation (221) is by (222)

$$= (A + C), \qquad (226)$$

and the sum of (202) and (203) is reduced by means of the equation

$$\text{sin.}^2\,a + \text{cos.}^2\,a = 1, \qquad (227)$$

to

$$A_1 + B_1 = A + C; \qquad (228)$$

and, therefore,

$A_1$ *and* $B_1$ *are the two roots* (222) *of the equation* (221).

146. *Corollary.* The value of $a$ may be obtained from the equation (217), which gives

$$\text{tang. } a = \frac{\text{sin. } a}{\text{cos. } a} = \frac{2\,(A_1 - A)}{B}, \qquad (232)$$

or it may be obtained directly from (206).

If we substitute in (206)

$$\text{sin.}\,(2a) = 2\,\text{sin.}\,a\,\text{cos.}\,a, \text{cos.}\,2\,a = \text{cos.}^2 a - \text{sin.}^2 a, \quad (233)$$

it becomes

$$(C - A)\,\text{sin.}\,2\,a + B\,\text{cos.}\,2\,a = 0; \qquad (234)$$

whence

$$\text{tang. } 2\,\alpha = \frac{\sin.\ 2\,\alpha}{\cos.\ 2\,\alpha} = \frac{B}{A-C}. \tag{235}$$

**147.** *Scholium.* The values of $A_1$ and $B_1$ (222) are always real as well as that of $\alpha$ (235), and those of $D_1$ and $E_1$ (204) and (205), and therefore the transformation from (199) to (201) is always possible. But the equations (209) (210) are impossible if $A_1$ and $B_1$ are both zero, while $D_1$ and $E_1$ are not zero, or if either $A_1$ or $B_1$ is zero, while the corresponding value $D_1$ or $E_1$ is not zero; so that in these cases the transformation from (201) to (207) is impossible.

**148.** *Scholium.* The values of $A_1$ and $B_1$ cannot both be zero, for, in this case, the quadratic terms would disappear from (201), and (201) could not, then, by art. 100, be a reduced form of a quadratic equation.

**149.** *Scholium.* If either $A_1$ or $B_1$ were zero, the corresponding root of (221) would be zero; that is, this equation would be satisfied by the value

$$X = 0,$$

which reduces it to

$$4\,AC - B^2 = 0; \tag{236}$$

and if we take $A_1$ for the root which vanishes, we have, by (232),

$$\text{tang. } \alpha = -\frac{2\,A}{B}. \tag{237}$$

But

$$\cos. \ \alpha = \frac{1}{\sec. \ \alpha} = \frac{1}{\sqrt{(1 + \tan.^2 \alpha)}}; \tag{238}$$

whence

$$\cos. \alpha = \frac{B}{\sqrt{(B^2 + 4\,A^2)}} \qquad (239)$$

$$\sin. \alpha = \cos. \alpha \,\tan\! g. \,\alpha = - \frac{2\,A}{\sqrt{(B^2 + 4\,A^2)}} \qquad (240)$$

$$D_1 = \frac{D\,B - 2\,A\,E}{\sqrt{(B^2 + 4\,A^2)}} \,; \qquad (241)$$

so that $D_1$ will also vanish, only when

$$D\,B = 2\,A\,E\,; \qquad (242)$$

and in this case (201) becomes

$$B_1\,y_1^2 + E_1\,y_1 + M = 0\,; \qquad (243)$$

which gives

$$y_1 = \frac{-E_1 \pm \sqrt{(E_1^2 - 4\,B_1\,M)}}{2\,B_1}\,; \qquad (244)$$

*so that the required locus is the combination of two lines drawn parallel to the axis of $x_1$ at the distances from it equal to these two values of $y_1$, unless these values are imaginary or equal, in the former of which cases there is no locus, and in the latter the given equation is the square of the equation of the line.*

150. *Scholium.* If the values of $A$, $B$, $C$ satisfy (236), so that one of the roots of (221) is zero, and if this one is taken for $A_1$, we have for the other root, by (222),

$$B_1 = \tfrac{1}{2}(A + C) + \tfrac{1}{2}\sqrt{(4\,A\,C + A^2 - 2\,A\,C + C^2)}$$
$$= \tfrac{1}{2}(A + C) + \tfrac{1}{2}(A + C) = A + C, \qquad (245)$$

10*

47

and (201) becomes

$$(A + C) y_1^2 + D_1 x_1 + E_1 y_1 + M = 0. \qquad (246)$$

The origin may now be transposed as in art. 143, the coördinates $a$ and $b$ being taken of such values that the coefficient of $y_2$ may be zero, and the sum of the terms which do not contain $x_2$ or $y_2$ may be zero, and (246) is thus reduced to

$$(A + C) y_2^2 + D_1 x_2 = 0. \qquad (247)$$

The values of $a$ and $b$ satisfy the equations

$$2 (A + C) b + E_1 = 0 \qquad (248)$$
$$(A + C) b^2 + D_1 a + E_1 b + M = 0, \qquad (249)$$

whence

$$b = - \frac{E_1}{2 (A + C)}$$
$$a = \frac{- (A + C) b^2 - E_1 b - M}{D_1};$$

and if we put

$$4 p = - \frac{D_1}{A + C}, \qquad (250)$$

(247) becomes

$$y_2^2 - 4 p x_2 = 0,$$
$$\text{or} \qquad y_2^2 = 4 p x_2. \qquad (251)$$

151. *Corollary.* If the equation (221) is written in the form

$$X^2 - (A + C) X + \tfrac{1}{4} (4 A C - B^2) = 0. \qquad (252)$$

The term $\tfrac{1}{4} (4 A C - B^2)$ is the product of the roots $A_1$ and $B_1$ of this equation.

$A_1$ and $B_1$ *are therefore of the same sign, when*

| Ellipse. | Point. |
|---|---|

**4** $AC$ *is greater than* $B^2$; *and they are of opposite signs if* 4 $AC$ *is less than* $B^2$.

**152.** *Corollary.* When $B^2$ is less than 4 $AC$, and, consequently, $A_1$ and $B_1$ are of the same sign, we will put

$$\frac{A_1}{\pm M_1} = \frac{1}{A_2^2}, \quad \frac{B_1}{\pm M_1} = \frac{1}{B_2^2}, \qquad (253)$$

that sign being prefixed to $M_1$, which renders the first members of these equations positive. If then (207) is divided by $\pm M_1$, the quotient is

$$\frac{x_2^2}{A_2^2} + \frac{y_2^2}{B_2^2} \pm 1 = 0. \qquad (254)$$

**153.** *Scholium.* If $M_1$ were zero, the equations (253) would be absurd, but in this case equation (207) would be

$$A_1 x_2^2 + B_1 y_2^2 = 0, \qquad (255)$$

in which both the terms of the first member have the sign, so that the equation can only be satisfied by the conditions

$$x_2 = 0, y_2 = 0, \qquad (256)$$

which represents the origin of the axes of $x_2$ and $y_2$.

Hence, and by art. 143, *the locus of the given equation is, in this case, the point whose coördinates are the values of a and b* (209) *and* (210).

**154.** *Scholium.* If $M_1$ were of the same sign with $A_1$ and $B_1$, the upper sign would be used in equations (253) and (254), the first member of (254) would then be the sum of three positive quantities, and could not be equal to zero.

*The given equation has, then, no locus, in this case.*

| Hyperbola. | Two lines. |
|---|---|

**155.** *Scholium.* When $M_1$ is of the sign opposite to that of $A_1$ and $B_1$, the lower sign must be used in equations (253) and (254), and (254) becomes, by transposition and omitting the numbers below the letters, which are no longer necessary,

$$\frac{x^2}{A^2} + \frac{y^2}{B^2} = 1, \qquad (257)$$

*which is of the same form with the equation* (69) *of the ellipse.*

**156.** *Corollary.* When $B^2$ is greater than $4\,AC$, and, consequently, $A_1$ and $B_1$ are of opposite signs, we will put

$$\frac{A_1}{\pm M_1} = \frac{1}{A_2^2}, \frac{B_1}{\pm M_1} = \frac{1}{B_2^2}, \qquad (258)$$

those signs being prefixed to $M_1$, which render the first members of these equations positive. If, then, (207) is divided by $\pm M_1$, the quotient is

$$\frac{x_2^2}{A_2^2} - \frac{y_2^2}{B_2^2} \pm 1 = 0. \qquad (259)$$

**157.** *Scholium.* If $M_1$ were zero, the equations (258) could not be used, but in this case equation (207) would be

$$A_1\, x_2^2 + B_1\, y_2^2 = 0,$$

which, multiplied by $A_1$, gives

$$A_1^2\, x_2^2 = -A_1\, B_1\, y_2^2\,;$$

or, extracting the root,

$$A_1\, x_2 = \pm \sqrt{(-A_1\, B_1)}\, y_2\,; \qquad (260)$$

the second member of which is real, because $A_1$ and $B_1$ are of opposite signs.

| Hyperbola. | Ellipse. |
|---|---|

*The locus of the given equation is then the combination of the two straight lines represented by the two equations included in* (260), *each of which passes through the origin of* $x_2$ *and* $y_2$.

158. *Scholium.* If $M_1$ is not zero, equation (259) may, by omitting the numbers below the letters and transposing the terms, be written in one of the forms

$$\frac{x^2}{A^2} - \frac{y^2}{B^2} = 1, \qquad (261)$$

or

$$\frac{y^2}{B^2} - \frac{x^2}{A^2} = 1; \qquad (262)$$

and the second of these equations becomes the same as the first by changing $x$, $y$, $A$, $B$ into $y$, $x$, $B$, $A$ respectively.

*Equation* (261) *is of the same form with equation* (85) *of the hyperbola.*

159. *Theorem.* The equation (257) is necessarily that of an ellipse.

*Proof.* To prove this, it is only necessary to show that each point of its locus is so situated, that the sum of its distances from two fixed points is always of the same length. By comparing the equation (257) with the solution of example 2, art. 98, it is apparent that, since all the points of the ellipse satisfy the equation (96,) they are in the required locus ; so that if, conversely, all the points of the required locus are in the ellipse, the two fixed points must be in the axis of $x$ at a distance $c$ from the origin such that

$$c = \pm \sqrt{(A^2 - B^2)}, \qquad (263)$$

and that the given length must be $2A$.

Now the distance $r$ of the point $x$, $y$ from one of these fixed points is, by (23),

$$r = \sqrt{[(x - c)^2 + y^2]};  \qquad (264)$$

but since $y^2 = B^2 - \dfrac{B^2 x^2}{A^2}$ and $c^2 = A^2 - B^2$,

we have

$$r = \sqrt{(x^2 - 2cx + c^2 + y^2)}$$

$$= \sqrt{\left(x^2 - 2cx - A^2 - \frac{B^2 x^2}{A^2}\right)}$$

$$= \sqrt{\left(\frac{A^2 - B^2}{A^2} x^2 - 2cx + A^2\right)}$$

$$= \sqrt{\left(\frac{c^2}{A^2} x^2 - 2cx + A^2\right)}$$

$$= \pm\left(\frac{cx}{A} - A\right) = \pm\frac{cx - A^2}{A}. \qquad (265)$$

Now of the two signs $+$ and $-$, that must be used which gives the distance $r$ positive. But we have

$$c < A \text{ and } x < A$$

for

$$c = \sqrt{(A^2 - B^2)}$$

and

$$x = \sqrt{\left(A^2 - \frac{A^2 y^2}{B^2}\right)}.$$

Hence

$$cx < A^2 \text{ or } cx - A^2 < 0; \qquad (266)$$

so that the lower sign must be used in (265), which gives

$$r = A - \frac{cx}{A}; \qquad (267)$$

so that for the distance from one of the fixed points we have

$$r_1 = A - \frac{x\sqrt{(A^2 - B^2)}}{A}, \qquad (268)$$

and for the distance from the other

$$r_2 = A + \frac{x\sqrt{(A^2 - B^2)}}{A}, \qquad (269)$$

whence $\qquad r_1 + r_2 = 2A; \qquad (270)$

that is, all the points of the required locus belong to the ellipse.

160. *Theorem.* The equation (261) is necessarily that of an hyperbola.

*Proof.* The proof is the same as in the preceding theorem, except that the word *difference* is to be used for *sum*, the sign of $B^2$ is to be changed, and in the value of $r$ (265) the upper sign is to be used, where $c$ and $x$ are both positive or both negative. For, since the values of $c$ and $x$ are

$$c = \pm\sqrt{(A^2 + B^2)} \text{ and } x = \pm\sqrt{\left(A^2 + \frac{A^2 y^2}{B^2}\right)}$$

we have, when $c$ and $x$ are of the same sign,

$$cx = \sqrt{(A^2 + B^2)} \cdot \sqrt{\left(A^2 + \frac{A^2 y^2}{B^2}\right)}$$

$$cx > A^2 \text{ or } cx - A^2 > 0;$$

whence $\qquad r_1 = \frac{cx}{A} - A. \qquad (271)$

But if $c$ and $x$ have opposite signs the product $cx$ is negative, so that

$$r_2 = \frac{cx}{A} + A, \qquad (272)$$

whence $\qquad$ $r_2 - r_1 = 2 A$; $\qquad$ (273)

that is, all the points of the required locus belong to the hyperbola.

161. *Theorem.* The equation (251) is necessarily that of a parabola.

*Proof.* Omitting the numbers written below the letters, we have only to show that the distance of each point of the locus from that point of the axis of $x$, whose distance from the origin is $p$, is equal to its distance from that line which is drawn parallel to the axis of $y$, and at the distance $-p$ from it. Now since the distance of the point $x$, $y$ from the axis of $y$ is $x$, its distance from the line parallel to it must be

$$x + p;$$

and its distance $r$ from the fixed point must be

$$r = \sqrt{[(x-p)^2 + y^2]}$$
$$= \sqrt{(x^2 - 2px + p^2 + 4px)} = \sqrt{(x^2 + 2px + p^2)}$$
$$= x + p, \qquad (274)$$

which is the same as the distance from the line; all the points of the locus of equation (251) are then upon the same parabola.

162. *Theorem.* In different ellipses which have the same transverse axis, the ordinates which correspond to the same abscissa are proportional to the conjugate axes.

*Proof.* Let the common transverse axis be $2\,A$, the different conjugate axes $2\,B$, $2\,B_1$, &c., and let the ordinates, which correspond to the same abscissa $x$, be $y$, $y_1$ &c. we have

$$A^2 y^2 = B^2 (A^2 - x^2)$$
$$A^2 y_1^2 = B_1^2 (A^2 - x^2),$$

whence, by division,

$$A^2 y^2 : A^2 y_1^2 = B^2 (A^2 - x^2) : B_1^2 (A^2 - x^2)$$

or $\qquad y^2 : y_1^2 = B^2 : B_1^2,$

or extracting the square root

$$y : y_1 = B : B_1 = 2B : 2B_1.$$

163. *Corollary.* Since the ellipse, whose conjugate axis is equal to its transverse axis, is a circle, the ordinate of an ellipse is to the corresponding ordinate of the circle, described upon the transverse axis as a diameter, as the conjugate axis is to the transverse axis.

164. *Corollary.* In different ellipses which have the same conjugate axis, the abscissas which correspond to the same ordinate are proportional to the transverse axes.

165. *Corollary.* The abscissa of an ellipse is to the corresponding abscissa of the circle, described upon the conjugate axis as a diameter, as the transverse axis is to the conjugate axis.

166. *Corollary.* It may be proved in the same way that in different hyperbolas, which have the same transverse axis, the ordinates which correspond to the same abscissa are proportional to the conjugate axes;

and that in different hyperbolas, which have the same conjugate axis, the abscissas, which correspond to the same ordinate, are proportional to the transverse axes.

167. *Corollary.* Understanding, by an *equilateral hyperbola*, one in which the axes are equal, the ordinate of any hyperbola is to the corresponding ordinate of the equilateral hyperbola, described upon its transverse axis, as the conjugate axis is to the transverse axis, and the abscissa of the hyperbola is to the corresponding abscissa of the equilateral hyperbola, described upon its conjugate axis, as the transverse axis is to the conjugate axis.

168. The term *abscissa* is often applied, in regard to the ellipse and hyperbola, to denote the distance of the foot of the ordinate from either of the extremities of the transverse axis.

Thus the abscissas of the point $M$ (fig. 38) of the ellipse are

$$CP = AC - AP = A - x$$

and
$$C'P = AC' + AP = A + x.$$

The abscissas of the point $M$ (fig. 36) of the hyperbola are

$$CP = AP - AC = x - A$$

and
$$C'P = AP + AC' = x + A.$$

169. *Theorem. The squares of the ordinates in an ellipse or hyperbola are proportional to the products of the corresponding abscissas*, the term abscissa being used in the sense of the preceding article.

---

*Proof.* I. The product of the abscissas for the point $x, y$ of the ellipse is, by the preceding article,

$$(A + x) (A - x) = A^2 - x^2;$$

and this product for the point $x', y'$ is

$$A^2 - x'^2.$$

But, by equation (68), we have

$$A^2 y^2 = A^2 B^2 - B^2 x^2$$
$$A^2 y'^2 = A^2 B^2 - B^2 x'^2;$$

whence

$$A^2 y^2 : A^2 y'^2 = A^2 B^2 - B^2 x^2 : A^2 B^2 - B^2 x'^2,$$

or, reducing to lower terms,

$$y^2 : y'^2 = A^2 - x^2 : A^2 - x'^2,$$

which is the proposition to be proved.

II. In the same way, for the hyperbola, the products of the abscissas for the points $x, y$, and $x', y'$ are

$$x^2 - A^2 \text{ and } x'^2 - A^2.$$

But, by equation (84),

$$A^2 y^2 = B^2 x^2 - A^2 B^2$$
$$A^2 y'^2 = B^2 x'^2 - A^2 B^2,$$

whence $\qquad y^2 : y'^2 = x^2 - A^2 : x'^2 - A^2.$

170. *Theorem. The squares of the ordinates in a parabola are proportional to the corresponding abscissas.*

*Proof.* For the point $x$, $y$ we have by (93)

$$y^2 = 4\,Px,$$

and for $x'$, $y'$ $\qquad y'^2 = 4\,Px',$

whence $\qquad y^2 : y'^2 = 4\,Px : 4\,Px' = x : x',$

which is the proposition to be proved.

**171. Problem.** To find the magnitude of an angle, which is inscribed in a semiellipse.

*Solution.* Let $CMC'$ (fig. 45) be the semiellipse, whose semiaxes are $A$ and $B$, let $I$ be the required angle $CMC'$, $\alpha$ the angle $MCX$, $\beta$ the angle $MC'X$, and $x'$, $y'$ the coördinates of the point $M$.

Because the line $MC$ passes through the point $x'$, $y'$ and the point $C$, whose coördinates are

$$y = 0, x = AC = A,$$

we have, by art. 121,

$$\text{tang. } \alpha = \frac{y'}{x' - A}; \qquad (275)$$

and, because the line $MC'$ passes through the point $x'$, $y'$ and the point $C'$, whose coördinates are

$$y = 0, \quad x = -A,$$

we have

$$\text{tang. } \beta = \frac{y'}{x' + A}; \qquad (276)$$

hence

$$\text{tang. } I = \text{tang } (\alpha - \beta) = \frac{\text{tang } \alpha - \text{tang. } \beta}{1 + \text{tang. } \alpha \text{ tang. } \beta}$$

$$= \frac{2\,A\,y'}{x'^2 - A^2 + y'^2}.$$

## Supplementary chords.

But, by (68),

$$x'^2 = \frac{A^2}{B^2}(B^2 - y'^2);$$

and, therefore,

$$\text{tang. } I = -\frac{2\,AB^2\,y'}{(A^2 - B^2)\,y'^2} = -\frac{2\,AB^2}{(A^2 - B^2)\,y'}. \quad (277)$$

172. *Corollary.* The product of (275) and (276) gives by the substitution of

$$y'^2 = \frac{B^2}{A^2}(A^2 - x'^2)$$

$$\text{tang. } \alpha \cdot \text{tang. } \beta = -\frac{B^2}{A^2}, \quad (278)$$

which is the condition that must be satisfied by the two angles $\alpha$ and $\beta$, in order that two lines $CM$ and $C'M$, drawn from the two points $C$ and $C'$, may meet upon the curve.

Two such lines are called *supplementary chords; so that* (278) *is the condition which expresses that two chords are supplementary.*

173. *Corollary.* If equation (278) is compared with (72), it is found to be identical with it; so that the condition that two chords are supplementary is identical with the condition that two diameters are conjugate.

*If then a given chord, as $CM$, is parallel to a given diameter $B_1AB'_1$, the chord $C'M$, supplementary to $CM$, is parallel to the diameter $C_1AC'_1$, conjugate to $B_1AB'_1$.*

174. *Problem. To draw a diameter, which is conjugate to a given diameter.*

11*

59

*Solution.* Let $B_1 A B'_1$, (fig. 45) be the given diameter. Through $C$ draw the chord $CM$ parallel to $B_1 A B'_1$; join $C'M$, and the diameter $C_1 A C'_1$, which is drawn parallel to $C'M$, is, by the preceding article, the required diameter.

**175. *Problem.*** To find the magnitude of the angle formed by two chords drawn from a point of the hyperbola to the extremities of its transverse axis, which are called *supplementary chords.*

*Solution.* The solution is the same as that of art. 177, except in regard to the sign of $B^2$, which being changed gives for the required angle $I$

$$\text{tang. } I = \frac{2\,A B^2}{(A^2 + B^2)\,y'}. \tag{279}$$

**176. *Corollary.*** The corollaries of arts. 172, 173, and the construction of art. 174, may then be applied to the hyperbola, and *equation* (88) *is the condition that two chords are supplementary.*

**177. *Theorem.*** The chords which are drawn parallel to the conjugate of any diameter of an ellipse or hyperbola are bisected by it.

*Proof.* For each value of $x$ there are two equal values of $y$, one positive the other negative, which are, in the ellipse,

$$y = \pm \frac{B}{A}\sqrt{(A^2 - x^2)}$$

and, in the hyperbola,

$$y = \pm \frac{B}{A}\sqrt{(x^2 - A^2)};$$

' so that if for the value of $x$ equal to $AP$ (fig. 46), the line
$MPM'$ is drawn parallel to the conjugate diameter, and if
$PM$, $PM'$ are taken each equal to the absolute value of $y$,
the points $M, M'$ are upon the curve, and the chord $MM'$,
which joins these points, is bisected at $P$.

178. *Corollary.* The same proposition and proof
may be applied to the parabola, using the word axis
instead of diameter.

179. *Corollary.* The chords drawn perpendicular to
either axis of an ellipse or hyperbola, or to the transverse axis of the parabola, are bisected by this axis.

180. *Problem.* To find the length of the chord
drawn through the focus of the ellipse, the hyperbola
or the parabola, perpendicular to the transverse axis;
this chord is called the *parameter of the curve.*

*Solution.* I. Represent the parameter of the ellipse by
$4p$; and its half or the ordinate is $2p$, the corresponding
abscissa being, by example 3, art. 98,

$$c = \sqrt{(A^2 - B^2)} \text{ or } c^2 = A^2 - B^2.$$

Hence the equation of the ellipse gives

$$2Ap = B\sqrt{(A^2 - c^2)} = B^2$$

$$2p = \frac{B^2}{A}, \quad 4p = \frac{2B^2}{A}.$$

II. In the same way in the hyperbola we should find the
same values of $2p$ and $4p$.

61

III. In the parabola whose equation is

$$y^2 = 4\,p\,x$$

the abscissa for the parameter is $p$; at which point

$$y^2 = 4\,p^2, y = 2\,p$$

$$\text{parameter} = 4\,p.$$

**181.** *Corollary.* In the ellipse or hyperbola, we have

$$A : B = B : 2\,p$$

or $\qquad 2\,A : 2\,B = 2\,B : 4\,p\,;$

so that *the parameter is a third proportional to the transverse and conjugate axes.*

**182.** *Theorem.* *The line drawn through either extremity of a diameter of the ellipse or hyperbola, parallel to the conjugate diameter, is a tangent to the curve.*

*Proof.* For the two values of $y$ are equal to zero at the point, so that neither of these lines has only one point in common with the curve.

**183.** *Problem.* *To draw a tangent to the ellipse or hyperbola at a given point of the curve.*

*Solution.* Join the given point $C_1$ to the centre $A$. Through the extremity $C$ of the transverse axis draw the chord $CM'$ parallel to $AC_1$. Join $C'M'$, and the line drawn through $C_1$ parallel to $C'M'$ is, by arts. 173 and 182, the required tangent.

**184.** *Scholium.* The drawing of tangents to these curves will be more fully discussed in a subsequent chapter.

**185.** *Problem.* To reduce the general equation of the second degree in space to its simplest form.

*Solution.* I. Substitute the equations (40, 41, 42) in (200), making

$$a = 0, \quad b = 0, \quad c = 0 ;$$

so that the direction of the axes may be changed without changing the origin.

If we represent the coefficients of $x_1^2$, $y_1^2$, $z_1^2$, $x_1$, $y_1$, $z_1$ by

$A_1 = A \cos.^2 \alpha + B \cos. \alpha \cos. \alpha' + C \cos.^2 \alpha'$

$\qquad + D \cos. \alpha \cos. \alpha'' + E \cos. \alpha' \cos. \alpha'' + F \cos.^2 \alpha''$

$B_1 = A \cos.^2 \beta + B \cos. \beta \cos. \beta' + C \cos.^2 \beta'$

$\qquad + D \cos. \beta \cos. \beta'' + E \cos. \beta' \cos. \beta'' + F \cos.^2 \beta''$

$C_1 = A \cos.^2 \gamma + B \cos. \gamma \cos. \gamma' + C \cos.^2 \gamma'$

$\qquad + D \cos. \gamma \cos. \gamma'' + E \cos. \gamma' \cos. \gamma'' + F \cos.^2 \gamma''$

$H_1 = H \cos. \alpha + I \cos. \alpha' + K \cos. \alpha''$

$I_1 = H \cos. \beta + I \cos. \beta' + K \cos. \beta''$

$K_1 = H \cos. \gamma + I \cos. \gamma' + K \cos. \gamma'',$

and take $\alpha, \beta, \gamma, \alpha', \beta', \gamma', \alpha'', \beta'', \gamma''$ to reduce the coefficients of $x_1 y_1$, $x_1 z_1$, $y_1 z_1$ to zero ; that is, to satisfy the equations

$0 = 2 A \cos. \alpha \cos. \beta + 2 C \cos. \alpha' \cos. \beta' + 2 F \cos. \alpha'' \cos. \beta''$

$\quad + B(\cos. \alpha \cos. \beta' + \cos. \alpha' \cos. \beta) + D(\cos. \alpha \cos. \beta''$

$\quad + \cos. \alpha'' \cos. \beta) + E(\cos. \alpha' \cos. \beta'' + \cos. \alpha'' \cos. \beta')$ (280)

$0 = 2 A \cos. \alpha \cos. \gamma + 2 C \cos. \alpha' \cos. \gamma' + 2 F \cos. \alpha'' \cos. \gamma''$

$\quad + B(\cos. \alpha \cos. \gamma' + \cos. \alpha' \cos. \gamma) + D(\cos. \alpha \cos. \gamma''$

$\quad + \cos. \alpha'' \cos. \gamma) + E(\cos. \alpha' \cos. \gamma'' + \cos. \alpha'' \cos. \gamma')$ (281)

$$0 = 2A \cos. \beta \cos. \gamma + 2C \cos. \beta' \cos. \gamma' + 2F \cos. \beta'' \cos. \gamma''$$

$$+ B (\cos. \beta \cos. \gamma' + \cos. \beta' \cos. \gamma) + D (\cos. \beta \cos. \gamma''$$

$$+ \cos. \beta'' \cos. \gamma) + E(\cos. \beta' \cos. \gamma'' + \cos. \beta'' \cos. \gamma'), \text{ (282)}$$

which, combined with the six equations (44 – 49), completely determine the values of these quantities, equation (200) becomes

$$A_1 x_1^2 + B_1 y_1^2 + C_1 z_1^2 + H_1 x_1 + I_1 y_1 + K_1 z_1 + M = 0. \text{ (283)}$$

II. Substitute the equations (53 – 55) for changing the origin to the axes $x_2$, $y_2$, $z_2$, and (283) becomes

$$A_1 x_2^2 + B_1 y_2^2 + C_1 z_2^2 + (2 A_1 a + H_1) x_2$$

$$+ (2 B_1 b + I_1) y_2 + (2 C_1 c + K_1) z_2 + M_1 = 0, \text{ (284)}$$

$$M_1 = A_1 a^2 + B_1 b^2 + C_1 c^2 + H_1 a + I_1 b + K_1 c + M,$$

and in which if $a$, $b$, $c$ are taken to satisfy the equations

$$2 A_1 a + H_1 = 0 \tag{285}$$

$$2 B_1 b + I_1 = 0 \tag{286}$$

$$2 C_1 c + K_1 = 0 \tag{287}$$

(284) becomes

$$A_1 x_2^2 + B_1 y_2^2 + C_1 z_2^2 + = M_1 0. \tag{288}$$

186. *Corollary.* If we take

$$L = 2 A \cos. \alpha + B \cos. \alpha' + D \cos. \alpha'' \tag{289}$$

$$L' = 2 C \cos. \alpha' + B \cos. \alpha + E \cos. \alpha'' \tag{290}$$

$$L'' = 2 F \cos. \alpha'' + D \cos. \alpha + E \cos. \alpha'. \tag{291}$$

These values may be substituted in (280), (281), and the double of the value of $A_1$, and they give

---

Quadratic equation in space.

---

$$2\,A_1 = L \cos. \, \alpha + L' \cos. \, \alpha' + L'' \cos. \, \alpha'' \quad (292)$$

$$0 = L \cos. \, \beta + L' \cos. \, \beta' + L'' \cos. \, \beta'' \quad (293)$$

$$0 = L \cos. \, \gamma + L' \cos. \, \gamma' + L'' \cos. \, \gamma''. \quad (294)$$

If (292) is multiplied by cos. $\alpha$, (293) by cos. $\beta$, and (294) by cos. $\gamma$, the coefficient of $L$ in the sum of the products is by (47) unity, while those of $L'$ and $L''$ are by (50) and (51) zero, so that this sum is by (289)

$$2\,A_1 \cos. \, \alpha = L = 2\,A \cos. \, \alpha + B \cos. \, \alpha' + D \cos. \, \alpha'', \; (295)$$

or $\quad 2\,(A_1 - A) \cos. \, \alpha - B \cos. \, \alpha' - D \cos. \, \alpha'' = 0. \; (296)$

If (292) is multiplied by cos. $\alpha'$, (293) by cos. $\beta'$, and (294) by cos. $\gamma'$, the sum of the products is, by (48, 50, 52, 290),

$$2\,A_1 \cos. \, \alpha' = L' = 2\,C \cos. \, \alpha' + B \cos. \alpha + E \cos. \, \alpha'', \; (297)$$

or $\quad 2\,(A_1 - C) \cos. \, \alpha' - B \cos. \, \alpha - E \cos. \, \alpha'' = 0. \quad (298)$

If (292) is multiplied by cos. $\alpha''$, (293) by cos. $\beta''$, and (294) by cos. $\gamma''$, the sum of the products is, by (49, 51, 52, 291),

$$2\,A_1 \cos. \, \alpha'' = L'' = 2\,F \cos. \alpha'' + D \cos. \, \alpha + E \cos. \alpha', \; (299)$$

or $\quad 2\,(A_1 - F) \cos. \, \alpha'' - D \cos. \, \alpha - E \cos. \, \alpha' = 0. \quad (300)$

If (296) is multiplied by $4\,(A_1 - C)\,(A_1 - F) - E^2$, (298) by $2\,B\,(A_1 - F) + D\,E$, (300) by $2\,D\,(A_1 - C) + BE$, the sum of the products divided by $2 \cos. \alpha$ is

$$4\,(A_1 - A)\,(A_1 - C)\,(A_1 - F) - E^2\,(A_1 - A)$$
$$- B^2\,(A_1 - F) - D^2\,(A_1 - C) - BDE = 0, \; (301)$$

from which the value of $A_1$ may be found.

---

---

187. *Corollary.* Since the value of $B_1$ is obtained from that of $A_1$ by changing $\alpha$, $\alpha'$, $\alpha''$ into $\beta$, $\beta'$, $\beta''$, and since by this same change and that of $\beta$, $\beta'$, $\beta''$ into $\gamma$, $\gamma'$, $\gamma''$, and also by that of $\gamma$, $\gamma'$, $\gamma''$ into $\alpha$, $\alpha'$, $\alpha''$, (280) is changed into (282), and (281) into (280) ; it follows that these same changes may be made in the equations from (295) to (301), and (301) will become

$$4(B_1 - A)(B_1 - C)(B_1 - F) - E^2(B_1 - A)$$
$$- B^2(B_1 - F) - D^2(B_1 - C) - BDE = 0, \quad (302)$$

from which $B_1$ may be found.

188. *Corollary.* Since the value of $C_1$ is obtained from that of $B_1$, by making the same changes as in the preceding article, and since, by these changes (282) is changed into (281), and (280) into (282) ; it follows that these changes may also be made in the equations obtained by the preceding article, (302) will thus become

$$4(C_1 - A)(C_1 - C)(C_1 - F) - E^2(C_1 - A)$$
$$- B^2(C_1 - F) - D^2(C_1 - C) - BDE = 0, \quad (303)$$

from which $C_1$ may be found.

189. *Corollary.* Since the equations for determining $A_1, B_1, C_1$ differ only in the letters which denote the unknown quantities, and since these equations are of the third degree, it is evident *that $A_1, B_1, C_1$ are the three roots of the equation of the third degree.*

$$4(X - A)(X - C)(X - F) - E^2(X - A)$$
$$- B^2(X - F) - D^2(X - C) - BDE = 0. \quad (304)$$

**190.** *Scholium.* Every equation of the third degree has at least one real root, so that one at least of the three quantities $A_1$, $B_1$, $C_1$ must be real. If we assume this one to be $A_1$, the corresponding values of cos. $\alpha$, cos. $\alpha'$, cos. $\alpha''$, determined by equations (296, 298, 300), and the 1st of art. 90, are also real; so that equations (280) and (281) are satisfied without assigning any values to $\beta$, $\beta'$, $\beta''$, $\gamma$, $\gamma'$, $\gamma''$. If (282) is not also satisfied, let its second member be represented by $D_1$, and equation (200), instead of being reduced to the form (283), will become

$$A_1 x_1^2 + B_1 y_1^2 + C_1 z_1^2 + D_1 y_1 z_1$$
$$+ H_1 x_1 + I_1 y_1 + K_1 z_1 + M = 0.$$

If now the same transformation is effected upon this equation, so as to transform it to the axes of $x_2$, $y_2$, $z_2$, the equation for determining $A_2$, $B_2$, $C_2$ would be obtained from (304), by changing $A$, $B$, $C$, $D$, $E$, $F$ into $A_1, 0, B_1, 0, D_1, C_1$, (304) thus becomes

$$4(X-A_1)(X-B_1)(X-C_1) - D_1^2(X-A_1) = 0, \quad (305)$$

the roots of which are

$$X = A_1,$$

and $\quad X = \frac{1}{2}(B_1 + C_1) \pm \frac{1}{2} \sqrt{[D_1^2 + (B_1 - C_1)^2]} \quad (306)$

which are all real, so that the given equation can always be transformed to the form (283), and all the roots of (304) will be real.

**191.** *Scholium.* If either $A_1$, $B_1$, or $C_1$ is zero, one of the equations (285 – 287) is impossible, unless the corresponding value of $H_1$, $I_1$, or $K_1$ is zero, and in this case the second transformation of § 185 is impossible.

**192.** *Scholium.* The three roots $A_1$, $B_1$, $C_1$ cannot all be

- 12

zero at the same time; for in this case (283) would be linear, and would not be a reduced form of a quadratic equation.

**193.** *Scholium.* If $A_1$ and $H_1$ are both zero, the values of $b$ and $c$ can be taken to satisfy equations (286) and (287), and (283) is then reduced to

$$B_1 \, y_2^2 + C_1 \, z_2^2 + M_1 = 0. \tag{307}$$

**194.** *Scholium.* If $A_1$ is zero and $H_1$ is not so, $b$ and $c$ can satisfy equations (286) and (287), and $a$ can be taken to satisfy the equation

$$M_1 = 0,$$

so that (283) is then reduced to

$$B_1 \, y_2^2 + C_1 \, z_2^2 + H_1 \, x_2 = 0. \tag{308}$$

**195.** *Scholium.* If $A_1$ and $B_1$ are zero, $c$ can be taken to satisfy equation (287), and if either $H_1$ or $I_1$ is not zero, $a$ or $b$ can be taken to satisfy the equation

$$M_1 = 0,$$

so that (283) is then reduced to

$$C_1 \, z_2^2 + H_1 \, x_2 + I_1 \, y_2 = 0. \tag{309}$$

But if both $H_1$ and $I_1$ are also zero, (283) becomes

$$C_1 \, z_2^2 + M_1 = 0. \tag{310}$$

**196.** *Scholium.* If the values of $A_1$, $B_1$, $C_1$, and $M_1$ have all the same sign, (288) is impossible, and *there is no locus.*

**197.** *Corollary.* If $A_1$, $B_1$, $C_1$ have all the same sign, which is the reverse of $M_1$, let $A_2$, $B_2$, $C_2$ be so taken, that

$$\frac{1}{A_2^2} = -\frac{A_1}{M_1}, \frac{1}{B_2^2} = -\frac{B_1}{M_1}, \frac{1}{C_2^2} = -\frac{C_1}{M_1}, \quad (311)$$

and the quotient of (288), divided by $-M_1$, is

$$\frac{x_2^2}{A_2^2} + \frac{y_2^2}{B_2^2} + \frac{z_2^2}{C_2^2} - 1 = 0. \quad (312)$$

**198.** *Corollary.* If two of the quantities $A_1$, $B_1$, $C_1$ have the same sign with $M_1$, while the other one, which we will assume to be $A_1$, has the reverse sign, we will take

$$\frac{1}{A_2^2} = -\frac{A_1}{M_1}, \frac{1}{B_2^2} = \frac{B_1}{M_1}, \frac{1}{C_2^2} = \frac{C_1}{M_1}, \quad (313)$$

and the quotient of (288), divided by $-M_1$, is

$$\frac{x_2^2}{A_2^2} - \frac{y_2^2}{B_2^2} - \frac{z_2^2}{C_2^2} - 1 = 0. \quad (314)$$

**199.** *Corollary.* If of the quantities $A_1$, $B_1$, $C_1$, one, namely $C_1$, has the same sign with $M_1$, while the other two have the reverse sign, we will take

$$\frac{1}{A_2^2} = -\frac{A_1}{M_1}, \frac{1}{B_2^2} = -\frac{B_1}{M_1}, \frac{1}{C_2^2} = \frac{C_1}{M_1}, \quad (315)$$

and the quotient of (288), divided by $-M_1$, is

$$\frac{x_2^2}{A_2^2} + \frac{y_2^2}{B_2^2} - \frac{z_2^2}{C_2^2} - 1 = 0. \quad (316)$$

**200.** *Corollary.* The values of $2\,A_2$, $2\,B_2$, $2\,C_2$ are called the *axes of the surface* in either of the three last articles, so that the three different values of

$$\sqrt{\left( \pm \frac{M_1}{X} \right)},$$

which are found from equation (304), are the *semi-axes*.

201. *Scholium.* If $M_1$ is zero, the equations (311), (313), and (315) are impossible, but in this case (288) becomes

$$A_1 \, x_2^2 + B_1 \, y_2^2 + C_1 \, z_2^2 = 0. \qquad (317)$$

202. *Scholium.* If $A_1$, $B_1$, and $C_1$ have all the same sign, (317) is only satisfied by the values

$$x_2 = 0, \quad y_2 = 0, \quad z_2 = 0, \qquad (318)$$

*so that the origin of $x_2$, $y_2$, $z_2$ is in this case the required locus.*

203. *Corollary.* If of the three quantities, $A_1$, $B_1$, $C_1$, one, as $C_1$, is negative, while the other two are positive, we will take

$$A_1 = \frac{1}{A_2^2}, \quad B_1 = \frac{1}{B_2^2}, \quad -C_1 = \frac{1}{C_2^2}, \qquad (319)$$

and (317) becomes

$$\frac{x_2^2}{A_2^2} + \frac{y_2^2}{B_2^2} - \frac{z_2^2}{C_2^2} = 0. \qquad (320)$$

204. The form of a surface is best investigated by examining the character of its curved sections, which

are made by different planes. The farther investigation of the surfaces, represented by quadratic equations, will, therefore, be reserved for Chapter IX.

### 205. EXAMPLES INVOLVING PLANE QUADRATIC LOCI.

I. To find the locus of all the points in a plane, which are so situated with regard to given points in that plane, that if the square of the distance of each point from the first given point is multiplied by $m'$, the square of its distance from the second given point by $m''$, &c., the sum of the products is equal to a given surface $V$.

*Solution.* Let the given points be, respectively, $x'$, $y'$; $x''$, $y''$, &c.

The distances of the point $x$, $y$ from these points is given by equation (23), and we have, by the conditions of the problem and using $S$, as in art. 141,

$$S \cdot m' (x - x')^2 + S \cdot m' (y - y')^2 = V,$$

or

$$S \cdot m' \cdot x^2 + S \cdot m' \cdot y^2 - 2 S \cdot m' x' \cdot x - 2 S \cdot m' y' \cdot y + S \cdot m' (x'^2 + y'^2) - V = 0.$$

This equation is already of the form (201), and may be reduced to the form (207) by making

$$a = \frac{S \cdot m' x'}{S \cdot m'}, \quad b = \frac{S \cdot m' y'}{S \cdot m'}$$

$$M_1 = \frac{-[(S \cdot m' x')^2 + (S m' \cdot y')^2]}{S \cdot m'}$$

$$+ S \cdot m' (x'^2 + y'^2) - V.$$

12*

We have then for the axes, by (253),

$$A_2 = \sqrt{\dfrac{-M_1}{S \cdot m'}} = B_2,$$

so that the locus is a circle, the coördinates of whose centre are $-a$ and $-b$, and whose radius is $A_2$.

*Corollary.* — $M_1$ and $S \cdot m'$ must be both positive or both negative.

2. To find the locus of all the points in a plane, which are so situated with regard to given lines in the plane, that if the square of the distance of each point from the first given line is multiplied by $m_1$, the square of its distance from the second line by $m_2$, &c., the sum of the products is equal to a given surface $V$.

*Solution.* Let the given lines be respectively

$$\sin. \, \alpha_1 \, x - \cos. \, \alpha_1 \, y = -p_1$$
$$\sin. \, \alpha_2 \, x - \cos. \, \alpha_2 \, y = -p_2, \&c.$$

The distances of the point $x$, $y$ of the locus from these lines is given by equation (170), and give, by the conditions of the problem, and using $S$ as before,

$$S \cdot m_1 \, (\sin. \, \alpha_1 \cdot x - \cos. \, \alpha_1 \cdot y + p_1)^2 = V,$$

which, developed and compared with equations (199–256), give $A_1$ and $B_1$ as the roots of the equation

$$4 X^2 - 4 \, S.m_1 \, X + 4 \, S.m_1 \sin.^2 \alpha_1 \, Sm_1 \cos.^2 \alpha_1 - (Sm_1 \sin.^2 \alpha_1)^2 = 0,$$

and to find $\alpha$,

$$\tan. \, 2 \, \alpha = \dfrac{S \cdot m_1 \sin. 2 \, \alpha_1}{S \cdot m_1 \cos. 2 \, \alpha_1},$$

and the values of $a, b, M_1$ may be found by equations (208–210).

3. To find the locus of the centres of all the circles which pass through a given point, and are tangent to a given line.

*Ans.* A parabola of which the given point is the focus, and the given line the directrix.

4. To find the locus of the centres of all the circles, which are tangent to two given circles.

*Ans.* When the locus is entirely contained within the given circles, it is an ellipse of which the foci are the two given centres, and the transverse axis is the difference of the two given radii, if both the contacts are internal; but the transverse axis is the sum of the radii if one of the contacts is internal while the other is external. Otherwise, it is an hyperbola, of which the foci are the two given centres, and the transverse axis the difference of the two given radii, if the contacts are both external or both internal, and their sum, if one of the contacts is external and the other internal; and it may be remarked, that the contact with either of the given circles is external upon one branch of the hyperbola, and internal upon the other.

# EQUATIONS OF THE SECOND DEGREE.

46. The general form for equations of the second degree, being those in which the ordinates $xy$ are involved to the second power, is

$$A x^2 + B y^2 + C x y + a x + b y + c = o$$

wherein each of the constants $A, B, C, a, b, c,$ may be either *positive* or *negative*,

Let us in the first place transfer the equation to two other rectangular axes parallel to the original ones and having their origin at a point whose ordinates are $a\,b$; and, (43,) by substituting $x + x'$ and $y + y'$ for $x$ and $y$, we shall find the corresponding equation to be

$$A\, (x^2 + 2 x' x + x'^2) + B\,(y^2 + 2 y' y + y'^2)$$
$$+ C\,(x y + y' x + x' y + x' y')$$
$$+ a\,(x + x') + b\,(y + y') + c = o ;$$

which arranged for $x$ and $y$ becomes

$$A x^2 + B y^2 + C x y$$
$$+ (2 A x' + C y' + a) x + (2 B y' + C x' + b) y$$
$$+ (A x'^2 + B y'^2 + C x' y' + a x' + b y' + c) = o,$$

47. The first three co-efficients $A, B, C$ stand unaffected with the new constants $x', y'$, by which we observe that they are independent of the position of the origin ; and hence the position of the origin of any equation of the second degree depends entirely on the values of the three last co-efficients $a\,b, c$.

48. We may now assume the values of the two ordinates $x'\,y'$ at pleasure since the position of the new origin is entirely arbitrary; and consequently, by the principles of algebra, we may fulfil any two possible conditions which involve them; let us therefore put the coefficients of $x$ and $y$ each equal to nothing, viz :

74

$$2\,A\,x' + C\,y' + a = 0,$$
$$2\,B\,y' + C\,x' + b = 0;$$

and thence

$$x' = \frac{C\,b - 2\,B\,a}{4\,A\,B - C^2}, \quad y' = \frac{C\,a - 2\,A\,b}{4\,A\,B - C^2};$$

hence also, by substitution, the last term

$$A\,x'^2 + B\,y'^2 + C\,x'y' + a\,x' + b\,y' + c = \frac{C\,a\,b - A\,b^2 - B\,a^2}{4\,A\,B - C^2} + c;$$

or by assuming

$$C\,a\,b - A\,b^2 - B\,a^2 + c\,(4\,A\,B - C^2) = G,$$

it becomes $=$

$$\frac{G}{4\,A\,B - C^2}.$$

The equation is thus transformed into

$$A\,x^2 + B\,y^2 + C\,x\,y + \frac{G}{4\,A\,B - C^2} = 0 \dots \ (a),$$

in which the fourth and fifth terms are wanting.

49. Let us now transfer this equation to two other rectangular axes inclined at an angle $\omega$ with the former and retaining the same origin; and, (44,) substituting $x \cos \omega - y \sin \omega$ and $x \sin \omega + y \cos \omega$ for $x$ and $y$, we get for the corresponding equation

$$A\,(x^2 \cos^2 \omega + y^2 \sin^2 \omega - 2\,x\,y \cos \omega \sin \omega)$$
$$+ B\,(x^2 \sin^2 \omega + y^2 \cos^2 \omega + 2\,x\,y \cos \omega \sin \omega)$$
$$+ C\,\{x^2 \cos \omega \sin \omega - y^2 \cos \omega \sin \omega + x\,y\,(\cos^2 \omega - \sin^2 \omega)\}$$
$$+ \frac{G}{4\,A\,B - C^2} = 0,$$

which arranged for $x$ and $y$, observing that

$$\cos^2 \omega - \sin^2 \omega = \cos 2\,\omega \text{ and } 2 \cos \omega \sin \omega = \sin 2\,\omega,$$

becomes

$$(A \cos^2 \omega + B \sin^2 \omega + C \cos \omega \sin \omega)\,x^2 + (A \sin^2 \omega + B \cos^2 \omega - C \cos \omega \sin \omega)\,y^2$$
$$+ \{C \cos 2\,\omega - (A - B) \sin 2\,\omega\}\,x\,y$$
$$+ \frac{G}{4\,A\,B - C^2} = 0,$$

By taking the value of $\omega$ so as to exterminate $xy$,
$$C \cos 2\omega - (A - B) \sin 2\omega = 0$$
$$\text{and } \tan 2\omega = \frac{C}{A - B};$$

which reduces the equation to
$$(A \cos^2 \omega + B \sin^2 \omega + C \cos \omega \sin \omega) \, x^2 + (A \sin^2 \omega + B \cos^2 \omega$$
$$- C \cos \omega \sin \omega) \, y^2$$
$$+ \frac{G}{4 \, A \, B - C^2} = 0;$$

and it hence appears that every line of the second order may be referred to two determinate rectangular axes so that its equation shall be transformed into the above form. By assuming
$$A \cos^2 \omega + B \sin^2 \omega + C \cos \omega \sin \omega = A',$$
$$A \sin^2 \omega + B \cos^2 \omega - C \cos \omega \sin \omega = B',$$
it becomes
$$A' \, x^2 + B' \, y^2 + \frac{G}{4 \, A \, B - C^2} = 0 \ldots (b).$$

50. Now if the principal semi-diameters of an ellipse and hyperbola be denoted by $a', b'$, and the former be taken for the axis of $x$ and the origin at the centre, their equations will be as follow :
For the ellipse
$$\frac{x^2}{a'^2} + \frac{y^2}{b'^2} = 1, \text{ or } b'^2 x^2 + a'^2 y^2 - a'^2 b'^2 = 0;$$
and for the hyperbola
$$\frac{x^2}{a'^2} - \frac{y^2}{b'^2} = \pm 1, \text{ or } b'^2 x^2 - a'^2 y^2 \mp a'^2 b'^2 = 0,$$

the under sign representing the conjugate hyperbola.
The signs may be all changed if necessary.
By means of these two equations and the foregoing transformed equation, $(b,)$ we deduce the following particulars relative to the general equation.

51. 1st. When $A', B'$ are both negative and $G$, $4 \, A B - C^2$ have the same sign, the equation determines an *ellipse ;* and

when $A'$, $B'$ are both of them positive and $G$ and $4\,AB - C'^2$ have different signs, the locus is also an *ellipse.*[*]

52. 2nd. When $A'$, $B'$ are of different signs and $G$ not $= o$, the locus is *an hyperbola.*

53. 3rd. In each of these cases the squares of the principal semi-diameters are equal to

$$\frac{\pm G}{A'(4\,AB - C^2)}, \quad \frac{\pm G}{B'(4\,AB - C^2)},$$

the under sign being for the ellipse and either sign for the hyperbola.

54. 4th. The values of $G, A', B'$ are determined from the equations

$$G = C\,ab - A\,b^2 - B\,a^2 + c\,(4\,AB - C^2) \ldots (1),$$

$$\tan 2\,\omega = \frac{C}{A - B} \ldots (2),$$

$$\left.\begin{array}{l} A' = A\cos^2 \omega + B\sin^2 \omega + C\cos \omega \sin \omega, \\ B' = A\sin^2 \omega + B\cos^2 \omega - C\cos \omega \sin \omega\,; \end{array}\right\} \ldots (3)$$

wherein $\omega$ is the angle included between the original axis of $x$ and the principal diameter of the curve.

55. 5th. The position of the centre of the curve is determined by

$$x' = \frac{Cb - 2Ba}{4\,AB - C^2}, \; y' = \frac{Ca - 2Ab}{4\,AB - C^2}.$$

56. 6th. When the equation is of the form

$$A\,x^2 + B\,y^2 + C\,xy + c = o,$$

wherein the fourth and fifth terms of the general equation are wanting, we have $a = o$, $b = o$ and thence $x' = o$, $y' = o$ which therefore shews the origin to be at the centre of the

---

[*] For the immediate values of $A'$, $B'$ see article 73.

curve. This agrees with equation ($b$,) article 49, where the origin is transferred to the centre.

57. 7th. By adding the equations (3), article 54, we find
$$A'' + B'' = A + B.$$
Hence we see that, whatever be the position of the axes of co-ordinates, the sum of the co-efficients of $x^2$ and $y^2$ will be the same.

58. 8th. When $G = o$ and also $A'$ and $B''$ of different signs, the general equation defines a straight line.
For in this case the transformed equation ($b$), article 49, becomes
$$A'' x^2 + B'' y^2 = o,$$
which gives
$$\frac{y}{x} = \sqrt{ -\frac{A''}{B''}};$$
and this value is real when $A''$, $B''$ have different signs.

59. 9th. In the two following cases it will be found that no real values of $x$ and $y$ can possibly fulfil the equation ($b$); and consequently that the equation can have no locus.
*First.* When $G$ and $4\,AB - C^2$ are of the same sign and $A''$, $B''$ both of them positive.
*Second.* When $G$ and $4\,AB - C^2$ are of different signs and $A''$, $B''$ are both negative.

60. 10th. When $G = o$ and $A''$, $B''$ have the same sign, no real values of $x$ and $y$ can satisfy the equation ($b$,) except the particular case of $x = o, y = o$. In this case therefore the locus is the single point corresponding with the new origin $x' y'$.

61. 11th. It appears that by changing the position of the origin to the centre $x' y'$
the equation
$$A\,x^2 + B\,y^2 + C\,xy + a\,x + b\,y + c = o$$

is transformed into the form
$$A x^2 + B y^2 + C x y + h = 0,$$
wherein $h = \dfrac{G}{4 A B - C^2}$.

Also, that by taking two other axes of co-ordinates making an angle with these so that $tan\, 2\,\omega = \dfrac{C}{A - B}$, the equation
$$A x^2 + B y^2 + C x y + h = 0$$
becomes of the form
$$A'' x^2 + B'' y^2 + h = 0$$
wherein $A'' + B'' = A + B$ and the constant $h$ is unchanged.

62. 12th. Let $x'', y''$ be the two semi-diameters of the curve
$$A x^2 + B y^2 + C x y + h = 0$$
which coincide with the axes of co-ordinates to which it is referred, and they will be determined by taking first $y = 0$ and then $x = 0$ in the equation, the results being
$$x''^2 = -\frac{h}{A}, \quad y''^2 = -\frac{h}{B}.$$

Let also $a', b'$ be the principal semi-diameters which coincide with the axes to which the equation
$$A'' x^2 + B'' y^2 + h = 0$$
appertains; and we similarly have
$$a'^2 = -\frac{h}{A''}, \quad b'^2 = -\frac{h}{B''}.$$
Hence as $A'' + B'' = A + B$, we have
$$\frac{1}{x''^2} + \frac{1}{y''^2} = \frac{1}{a'^2} + \frac{1}{b'^2};$$

That is the sum of the reciprocals of the squares of any two semi-diameters, of a curve of the second order, which are perpendicular to each other, is the same; and, in reference to the general equation, is $=$
$$-\frac{A + B}{h} = -\frac{A + B}{G} (4 A B - C^2).$$

**63.** When $4AB - C^2 = o$, we have, (55), $x'y'$ both of them *infinite* which shews the centre of the curve to be infinitely remote from the origin. It becomes hence necessary to consider this case separately.

Let

$$A x^2 + B y^2 + C x y + a x + b y + c = o$$

be the general equation in which $4 AB - C^2 = o$.

Then, transferring the origin to a point $x' y'$, the corresponding equation, (46,) is

$$A x^2 + B y^2 + C x y$$
$$+ (2 A x' + C y' + a) x + (2 B y' + C x' + b) y$$
$$+ (A x'^2 + B y'^2 + C x' y' + a x' + b y' + c) = o.$$

Let $x' y'$ determine some point in the curve, so that

$$A x'^2 + B y'^2 + C x' y' + a x' + b y' + c = o,$$

and the equation becomes

$$A x^2 + B y^2 + C x y$$
$$+ (2 A x' + C y' + a) x + (2 B y' + C x' + b) y = o.$$

But, since $4 AB - C^2 = o$ and $\therefore C = 2 \sqrt{AB}$, we have

$$A x^2 + B y^2 + C x y = (x \sqrt{A} + y \sqrt{B})^2.$$

Hence the reduced equation is equivalent to

$$(x \sqrt{A} + y \sqrt{B})^2$$
$$+ (2 A x' + C y' + a) x + (2 B y' + C x' + b) y = o.$$

**64.** We shall now, as in article 49, transfer this equation to two other rectangular axes proceeding from the same origin and making an angle $\omega$ with the former; and, (44,) putting $x \cos \omega - y \sin \omega$ and $x \sin \omega + y \cos \omega$ for $x$ and $y$, the resulting equation is

$$\{(\cos \omega \sqrt{A} + \sin \omega \sqrt{B}) x - (\sin \omega \sqrt{A} - \cos \omega \sqrt{B}) y\}^2$$
$$+ \{(2 A x' + C y' + a) \cos \omega + (2 B y' + C x' + b) \sin \omega\} x$$
$$- \{(2 A x' + C y' + a) \sin \omega - (2 B y' + C x' + b) \cos \omega\} y = o.$$

Let $\omega$ satisfy the condition

$$\cos \omega \sqrt{A} + \sin \omega \sqrt{B} = o,$$

which will give

$$\tan \omega = - \sqrt{\frac{A}{B}}, \cos \omega = - \sqrt{\frac{B}{A+B}}, \sin \omega = \sqrt{\frac{A}{A+B}};$$

E

80

and thence

$$\sin \omega \sqrt{A} - \cos \omega \sqrt{B} = \sqrt{(A+B)};$$

$$(2Ax'+Cy'+a)\cos\omega+(2By'+Cx'+b)\sin\omega=-\frac{a\sqrt{B}-b\sqrt{A}}{\sqrt{(A+B)}}$$

and $(2Ax'+Cy'+a)\sin\omega-(2By'+Cx'+b)\cos\omega=$

$$2x'\sqrt{A(A+B)}+2y'\sqrt{B(A+B)}+\frac{a\sqrt{A}+b\sqrt{B}}{\sqrt{(A+B)}}$$

$$=2\sqrt{(A+B)}\left\{x'\sqrt{A}+y'\sqrt{B}+\frac{a\sqrt{A}+b\sqrt{B}}{2(A+B)}\right\}.$$

The equation thus becomes

$$(A+B)y^2-\frac{a\sqrt{B}-b\sqrt{A}}{\sqrt{(A+B)}}x$$

$$-2\sqrt{(A+B)}\left\{x'\sqrt{A}+y'\sqrt{B}+\frac{a\sqrt{A}+b\sqrt{B}}{2(A+B)}\right\}y=0.$$

65. We have, (63,) assumed $x'y'$ to determine a point in the curve, but not restricted ourselves to any particular point; we may therefore take this point where the curve is intersected by a straight line whose equation is

$$x\sqrt{A}+y\sqrt{B}+\frac{a\sqrt{A}+b\sqrt{B}}{2(A+B)}=a,$$

by means of which we shall have

$$x'\sqrt{A}+y'\sqrt{B}+\frac{a\sqrt{A}+b\sqrt{B}}{2(A+B)}=0,$$

which reduces the equation to

$$(A+B)y^2-\frac{a\sqrt{B}-b\sqrt{A}}{\sqrt{(A+B)}}.x=0,$$

or $y^2-\dfrac{a\sqrt{B}-b\sqrt{A}}{(A+B)^{\frac{3}{2}}}.x=0\ldots.(c).$

But the equation of a parabola, whose parameter is $p$, taking the origin at the vertex and the principal axis for the axis of $x$, is

$$y^2=px \text{ or } y^2-px=0.$$

Hence the following particulars:—

66. 1st. When $a\sqrt{B}-b\sqrt{A}$ not $=0$, the locus is a *Parabola* whose parameter is equal to

81

$$\frac{a \sqrt{B} - b \sqrt{A}}{(A+B)^{\frac{3}{2}}}.$$

67. 2nd. According to article 12, the equation

$$x \sqrt{A} + y \sqrt{B} + \frac{a \sqrt{A} + b \sqrt{B}}{2(A+B)} = o$$

defines a straight line inclined to the original axis of $x$ at an angle whose tangent $= - \sqrt{\frac{A}{B}}$ and which is therefore equal to $\omega$, the inclination of the axis of the curve, with the axis of $x$; this line, (65,) also passing through the vertex $x'y'$, it must coincide with the axis of the curve. Therefore the above equation properly represents the *principal diameter* of the curve; by uniting it with the original equation we may hence find the co-ordinates $x'y'$ of its intersection with the curve, or the vertex.

68. 3rd. If $a \sqrt{B} - b \sqrt{A} = o$, or $a \sqrt{B} = b \sqrt{A}$, the equation (c) gives simply

$$y = o,.$$

which shews the locus in this case to be a straight line corresponding with the new axis of $x$, the equation of which is given, (67).

69. 4th. The equation $4AB - C^2 = o$ giving $C^2 = \pm 2 \sqrt{AB}$, the values of the constants $A, B$ must have the same sign to make $C$ real, that is, they must be either both of them positive or both negative; and hence we may consider them both positive for, when negative, they can be made so by preliminarly changing all the signs of the original equation. If, under this consideration, $C$ be negative we shall have $C = - 2 \sqrt{AB}$ instead of $+ 2 \sqrt{AB}$; in this case, the foregoing operations hold good by either substituting $- \sqrt{A}$ instead of $\sqrt{A}$ or $- \sqrt{B}$ for $\sqrt{B}$, or by considering either $\sqrt{A}$ or $\sqrt{B}$ to have a negative value; and $\tan \omega$ will become hence $= + \sqrt{\frac{A}{B}}$ instead of $- \sqrt{\frac{A}{B}}$.

Thus we see that, when $C$ is *negative, tan* $\omega$ *is positive* and $\omega < \frac{\pi}{2}$; and that, when $C$ is *positive, tan* $\omega$ is *negative* and $\therefore \omega > \frac{\pi}{2}$.

The foregoing investigations lead immediately to the solutions of the three following propositions:

70. *To express the equations of the principal diameters of a curve of the second order which is determined by the general equation.*

The co-ordinates of the centre, (55,) are

$$x' = \frac{Cb - 2Ba}{4AB - C^2}, \; y' = \frac{Ca - 2Ab}{4AB - C^2}.$$

Let $\omega$ denote the inclination of one of the principal diameters of the curve with the co-ordinate axis of $x$; and, (54,)

$$\tan 2\omega = \frac{C}{A - B},$$

from which

$$\tan\omega = \frac{\sec 2\omega - 1}{\tan 2\omega} = \frac{\sqrt{\{(A-B)^2 + C^2\}} - (A-B)}{C}.$$

Now the diameter being inclined to the co-ordinate axis of $x$ at the angle $\omega$ and also passing through the centre $x'y'$ of the curve, its equation, (22,) is

$$y - y' = (x - x') \tan\omega.$$

Hence by substitution we have

$$y - \frac{Ca - 2Ab}{4AB - C^2} =$$

$$\left(x - \frac{Cb - 2Ba}{4AB - C^2}\right). \frac{\sqrt{\{(A-B)^2 + C^2\}} - (A-B)}{C} \dots (x),$$

for the equation of one of the principal diameters.

The other diameter passing through the centre $x'y'$ perpendicular to this, its equation, (36,) is

$$y - \frac{Ca - 2Ab}{4AB - C^2} =$$

$$-\left(x - \frac{Cb - 2Ba}{4AB - C^2}\right). \quad \frac{C}{\sqrt{\{(A-B)^2 + C^2\}} - (A-B)}$$

or, which is the same,

$$y - \frac{Ca - 2Ab}{4AB - C^2} =$$

$$-\left(x - \frac{Cb - 2Ba}{4AB - C^2}\right). \frac{\sqrt{\{(A-B)^2 + C^2\}} + (A-B)}{C} \dots (y).*$$

**71. Cor. 1.** If the origin of the ordinates be the centre of the curve its equation, (56,) will be of the form

$$A x^2 + B y^2 + C x y + c = 0;$$

and we shall have $a = o, b = o$. In this case therefore the equations of the principal diameters are

$$y = \frac{\sqrt{\{(A-B)^2 + C^2\}} - (A-B)}{C}. x$$

and

$$y = - \frac{\sqrt{\{(A-B)^2 + C^2\}} + (A-B)}{C}. x$$

**72. Note.** The equation

$$\tan 2\omega = \frac{C}{A-B}$$

applies equally to both diameters. For, if $2\omega$ fulfil this equation, it will also hold good when $2\omega \pm \pi$ is substituted; and, $\omega$ denoting the inclination of one of the diameters, $\omega \pm \frac{\pi}{2}$ will evidently be that of the other.

From this equation we derive generally

$$\tan \omega = \frac{\sec 2\omega - 1}{\tan 2\omega} = \pm \frac{\sqrt{\{(A-B)^2 + C^2\}} - (A-B)}{C},$$

the upper sign appertaining to one of the axes and the under sign to the other.

---

* By uniting these equations of the principal diameters with the given equation of the curve we may thence find the positions of the vertices.

Thus, by making use of the under sign, the equation $(x)$ will become the same as the equation $(y)$, and vice versâ ——, because

$$-\frac{\sqrt{\{(A-B)^2+C^2\}}-(A-B)}{C} \cdot \frac{\sqrt{\{(A-B)^2+C^2\}}-(A-B)}{C}$$

$$=-1.$$

When $4AB-C^2=o$, see article 67.

73. *The equation of a curve of the second order being given to find the values of its principal semi-diameters.*

The squares of the semi-diameters are, (53,) equal to

$$\frac{+G}{A''(4AB-C^2)}, \quad \frac{+G}{B''(4AB-C^2)},$$

wherein, (54,)

$$G = Cab - Ab^2 - Ba^2 + c(4AB-C^2);$$
$$A'' = A\cos^2\omega + B\sin^2\omega + C\cos\omega\sin\omega,$$
$$B'' = A\sin^2\omega + B\cos^2\omega - C\cos\omega\sin\omega,$$

and $\tan 2\omega = \dfrac{C}{A-B}$.

From the last we deduce

$$\cos^2\omega = \frac{1}{2}\left(1+\frac{1}{\sec 2\omega}\right) = \frac{1}{2}\left(1+\frac{A-B}{\sqrt{\{(A-B^2)+C^2\}}}\right),$$

$$\sin^2\omega = \frac{1}{2}\left(1-\frac{1}{\sec 2\omega}\right) = \frac{1}{2}\left(1-\frac{A-B}{\sqrt{\{(A-B)^2+C^2\}}}\right)$$

$$\cos\omega\sin\omega = \frac{C}{2\sqrt{\{(A-B)^2+C^2\}}},$$

and hence we get

$$A'' = \frac{A+B+\sqrt{\{(A-B)^2+C^2\}}}{2},$$

$$B'' = \frac{A+B-\sqrt{\{(A-B)^2+C^2\}}}{2}.$$

These and the foregoing value of $G$ substituted, the squares

85

of the principal semi-diameters of the curve are found equal to

$$\pm \frac{2\{Cab - Ab^2 - Ba^2 + c(4AB - C^2)\}}{(4AB - C^2)\left[A + B + \surd\{(A-B)^2 + C^2\}\right]},$$

$$\pm \frac{2\{Cab^2 - Ab^2 - Ba^2 + c(4AB - C^2)\}}{(4AB - C^2)\left[A + B - \surd\{(A-B)^2 + C^2\}\right]},$$

the under sign being for the ellipse and either sign for the hyperbola, (53.)

74. When the origin is at the centre of the curve, (61,) $a = o, b = o$; and therefore in this case the squares of the principal semi-diameters are equal to

$$\frac{+2c}{A + B + \surd\{(A-B)^2 + C^2\}}, \quad \frac{+2c}{A + B - \surd\{(A-B)^2 + C^2\}}.$$

75. *To determine the particular description of a curve of the second order from the immediate relative values of the constants which belong to its equation.*

In (51), (52) and the subsequent articles, the different cases are severally stated, throughout the various relations of $A'', B'', G, 4AB - C^2$, &c., where $A'', B''$ are, (54,) expressed in terms of the coefficients $A, B, C$, by means of the arc $\omega$ as a subsidiary. It is hence only necessary to transfer the relations of $A'', B''$ to those of the immediate coefficients $A, B, C$, which may be easily effected from their values which have already been found, (73,) viz:

$$A'' = \frac{A + B + \surd\{(A-B)^2 + C^2\}}{2},$$

$$B'' = \frac{A + B - \surd\{(A-B)^2 + C^2\}}{2}.$$

Thus it is evident that, when $(A+B)^2$ is greater than $(A-B)^2 + C^2$ the sign of $A+B$ cannot be affected with either the

addition or subtraction of $\sqrt{\{(A-B)^2+C^2\}}$, and consequently that the values of $A', B'$ will both have the same
sign with $A+B$. But, when $(A+B)^2$ is greater than
$(A-B)^2+C^2$, we shall have $(A+B)^2-\{(A-B)^2+C^2\}=$
$4AB-C^2$ positive. Hence, when $4AB-C^2$ is positive
$A'$ and $B'$ will both of them have the same sign with $A+B$,
that is, they will both be positive when $A+B$ is positive and
both negative when $A+B$ is so.

It is also pretty obvious that, when $(A+B)^2$ is less than
$(A-B)^2+C^2$, the values of $A'B'$ will have different signs,
that is, the one will be positive and the other negative.
In this case we shall have $(A+B)^2-\{(A-B)^2+C^2\}=$
$4AB-C^2$ negative. Thus we see, when $4AB-C^2$ is
negative, that $A', B'$ are of different signs.*

Again, under the class $4AB-C^2=o$, when the value of
$a\sqrt{B}-b\sqrt{A}=o$, we shall have $2\sqrt{A}(a\sqrt{B}-b\sqrt{A})$
$=2a\sqrt{AB}-2Ab=o$
$$\text{or } Ca-2Ab=o.$$

Hence also, when $a\sqrt{B}-b\sqrt{A}$ not $=o$, we shall have
$Ca-2Ab$ not $=o$.

By carefully comparing these relations with the articles
(51), (52), (58), (59), (60), (66), and (68), we find the different
descriptions of the curve to be as in the following arrange-
ment, wherein
$$G=Cab-Ab^2-Ba^2+c(4AB-C^2).$$

---

* These relations are also pretty evident from the equations
$$A'+B'=A+B,$$
$$4A'B'=4AB-C^2.$$

When $4AB - C^2$ is positive; and $A + B$ and $G$ are of *different signs*, the locus is *an* ELLIPSE.

............................. are of *the same signs*,........... IMPOSSIBLE.

————— and $G = 0$, ............................. *a* POINT.

—————— is *negative*; ............... $G$ *not* $= 0$, ................. *an* HYPERBOLA.

............................. $G = 0$, .................................... *a* STRAIGHT LINE.

......$4AB - C^2 = 0$ .....; and $Ca - 2Ab$ *not* $= 0$, ............... *a* PARABOLA.

.............................; ...... $Ca - 2Ab = 0$, .................. *a* STRAIGHT LINE.

*Note.*——When the origin of the axes is at the centre of the curve and consequently the equation is

$$Ax^2 + By^2 + Cxy + c = 0,$$

the value of $G$ is simply $c\,(4AB - C^2)$.

Printed in the USA
CPSIA information can be obtained
at www.ICGtesting.com
LVHW041217310823
756836LV00003B/683

9 781447 456711